FORBIDDEN FRUIT

FORBIDDEN FRUIT

On the Relationship Between Women and Knowledge
in
Doris Lessing
Selma Lagerlöf
Kate Chopin
Margaret Atwood

by

Bonnie St. Andrews

The Whitston Publishing Company
Troy, New York
1986

Library of Congress Catalog Card Number 85-52169

ISBN 0-87875-308-7

Printed in the United States of America

Dedication

All waits or goes by default till a strong being appears;
A strong being is the proof of the race and of the ability
of the universe.
When he or she appears materials are overaw'd,
The dispute on the soul stops,
The old customs and phrases are confronted, turn'd back, or
laid away.

"Songs of the Broad Axe"
-Walt Whitman-

To My Strong Beings:

Anne Boyer St. Andrews
&
Wally St. Andrews

Contents

Preface

Apologia as Invitation

For those engaged in the study of Literature, the desire for "knowledge of good and evil" is a fundamental issue. More has been written about this primordial plucking of the "forbidden fruit"—and its consequences—than about any single act since. Unsurprisingly, then, this presentation examines the continuing human dilemma created by the desire for knowledge of good and evil. In the Judeo-Christian culture, this desire is severely disapproved.

Judging this act punishable continues to restrict human access to knowledge in peculiar ways. Such restrictions are usually applied to females rather than to males. While mindful that knowledge knows no gender, Judeo-Christian tradition generally indicts Eve as the "author of our woes" and cause of our collective "fall." Whether that fall is fortunate or unfortunate remains debatable; that Eve should be castigated for disobeying the command forbidding knowledge of good and evil is, however, generally agreed.

Learning that Prometheus can steal fire and be lionized but that Eve can steal knowledge and be vilified subtly skews human attitudes towards men who disobey the gods and women who disobey the gods.* Those Pauline injunctions that women "be under obedience" and that "if they will learn anything let them ask their husbands at home" not only sanctify the sexual imbalance of power but also control women's access to knowledge. The male (mortal or divine) decides what the female

---

* Prometheus receives knowledge from Athena; curiously enough, his punishment for theft is being given Pandora, another archetypally curious—ergo dangerous—female.

needs to know.

Such programming influences the development of many faculties. This situation invites, to choose the politest possible word, re-examination. To many among the sexually enlightened, those proscriptions of Paul and many churches's Fathers seem ludicrous; nevertheless, such attitudes pervade culture. They influence all of us in insidious ways. Long after the barrage against Fundamentalist interpretations of Genesis, men and women conform to the traditionally ascribed roles (curses) "ordained" for the sexes.

Sexual shame, distrust of female initiative, sovereignty of males, the division of carnal knowledge from knowledge of good and evil, fear of mutual betrayal all find sanction in the approved interpretations of Eve's disobedience, of Adam's compliance. Therefore, how men and women approach this desire for knowledge of good and evil remains problematic. In short, these attitudes, which influence the ethical development of the race, seem pernicious.

In sacred tales and secular stories (myths and fairytales) women are cautioned against wanting knowledge. This act is deemed willful, disobedient and perilous. The "curious" woman—Pandora, Psyche, Eve—provokes divine displeasure by seeking knowledge, bringing disgrace upon herself and calumny to others. Mircea Eliade notes that in these cosmogonical myths, the social order finds spiritual ordination:

> . . . all the primordial events in consequence of which man [sic] became what he is today—mortal, sexed, organized in a society, obliged to work in order to live, and to work in accordance with certain rules.[1]

This inventories, in social terms, the curses listed in Genesis; human attitudes seem riveted to such archaic and, putatively, immutable laws.

Given this inculcated fear of women's choosing knowledge of good and evil, the act remains a daring one. This analysis examines four females in the act of choosing such "forbidden fruit." Their insights, obstacles, discoveries indicate the variety of the female experience of knowledge of good and evil. The novels chosen are *The Treasure* by the 1909 winner of the Nobel Prize for Literature, Selma Lagerlöf; *The Awakening* (1899) by the re-acclaimed Kate O'Flaherty Chopin; *Surfacing*

(1973) by Canada's Margaret Atwood, prolific poet, critic, and novelist who has won the coveted Governor-General's Award; *The Summer Before the Dark* (1973) by Britain's Doris Lessing, author of the monumental Martha Quest series.

While this presentation certainly examines how the daughters of Eve respond to the "forbidden fruit," the desire for knowledge is, assuredly, a human one. The individual's confrontation with knowledge is as singular as circumstance and personality can design. Sacred and secular literatures abound with protagonists who—willingly or unwillingly—confront knowledge and undergo radical change. Thus, Oedipus seeks to know and suffers the ethical consequences of that knowing. Saul, struck down by ineluctable enlightenment, rises as Paul.

Obviously, the encounter with knowledge alters identity itself on such basic levels as belief, aspiration, roles, and responsibilities. In these novels, too, the encounter with knowledge is transforming; each protagonist calls into question all the socio-spiritual definitions of good and evil. In the process, each undergoes a real and metaphorical exile from former gardens, former identities.

What connects these disparate works is an underlying technique of defining the female in terms of mythic and fairy-tale expectations and proscriptions. While the novels employ different forms (Lagerlöf's is a saga, Chopin's a domestic novel, Lessing's a novel of manners, and Atwood's a psychological novel), each manipulates mythic/fairytale elements into the structure of the novel to show how the female is forbidden knowledge and how she re-defines herself despite the confines of such female identity patterns.

To help readers unfamiliar with such patterns or these technical aspects, this analysis includes references to literatures of various countries, genres, and genders. These allusions should provide safe passage over what are only mirage chasms: women's issues, women's literature. Those untutored in literature written by women can rely on the technical signposts which guide all good literature, and this remark is not made facetiously.

That we have gender-identified literature seems preposterous to many writers, to many readers. That a particular work must reflect its culture—be that a Jewish or Black or Female one—seems useful and meritorious, to a point. When, however, the possibility of that literature's having universal merit is undercut by such categorization, the point becomes a blunt instrument.

That literature written by a Black or a Woman must bear its descriptive adjective bothers many of us because the diversity, achievement, and power of Literature seem thus stunted, impoverished, reduced.

Perhaps all writers write for nothing less than Eternity; perhaps in the very act of describing confines or conditions of class, place, gender, race, the writer jumps over these railroad gates, then over the multifarious moon. Walt Whitman hardly sings the exultant "Song of Myself" for only his time and countrymen/women. Nor does Zora Neale Hurston compose *Jonah's Gourd Vine* for Black males named Jonah.

This issue of the relationship to knowledge is human and ethical. As Carl Sagan notes in *The Dragons of Eden,* this prohibition against "not the getting of any sort of knowledge, but, specifically, the knowledge of good and evil," relates to that part of the brain connected with ethical decision-making.[2] How the twenty-first century judges Eve's action, is therefore, an ethical issue with profound ramifications. In an affirming mode, this work invites re-consideration by those willing to consider the diverse and as yet restricted conjunctions between women and knowledge.

This study—and others in our prolonged and pivotal quest for woman's untainted right to knowledge and its concomitant, power,—owes a debt to those who went before. Two major writers, Elizabeth Cady Stanton for her *The Woman's Bible* (1895-98) and Matilda Joslyn Gage for her *Woman, Church and State* (1893), merit continuing thanks and praise.

This determination for ethical self-rule is quintessential to the evolution of the race: humans striving for ethical progress must consider "the woman question." We must, women and men, slay the dragons, despite their age and entrenched power:

> The woman who possesses love for her sex, for the world,
> for truth, justice and right, will not hesitate to place
> herself upon record as opposed to falsehood, no matter
> under what guise or holiness it appears.[3]

Notes

[1] Mircea Eliade, *Myth and Reality* (New York: Harper & Row, Publishers, 1963), p. 11.

[2] Carl Sagan, *The Dragons of Eden,* (New York: Ballantine Books, 1979), p. 147. In this desire to fuse what Sagan calls the "religious and scientific mythologies," he follows an eminent line of thinkers from Gosse to Huxley to Cady-Stanton.

[3] Matilda Joslyn Gage, *Woman, Church and State,* (Watertown, MA: Persephone Press, 1980), p. 245.

Mythos

In the beginning was "the Word," and word got around that Eve had enjoyed a peculiar relationship with a highly symbolic, deeply metaphorical, utterly delectable apple. That fruit—be it apple, pomegranate, quince—represents "knowledge of good and evil." And the fruit, alas, was forbidden. As all readers of Genesis or Snow White can attest, such fruit is, spiritually if not physically, poisonous. Seeking "knowledge of good and evil" is a punishable act; the quest earns the quester ignominy. Indeed, it is difficult to find any good at all in the usual interpretation of this act.

In myths and stories—sacred and secular tales—women and knowledge seem the fateful conjunction. Because Eve—the first obtainer of "knowledge of good and evil"—is so thoroughly vilified for this undertaking, the entire enterprise would seem to suffer irremedial damage as a goal. Or, at the very least, this disobedience might seem incontrovertibly negative from this time-before-time on. But this is not quite accurate.

Literature repeatedly celebrates disobedience and the quest for "knowledge of good and evil." Of course, the celebration seems slanted according to which sex seeks knowledge. For example, mythic and willful women—Eve, Pandora, Psyche—are usually abhorred for such acts. The female seeking knowledge, if she is not vituperated outright, is ridiculed or demeaned as "curious." The curious woman, like the curious cat, places herself almost mindlessly in harm's way to satisfy an idle yearning. But the desire for this "knowledge of good and evil" is not deemed unworthy.

In fact, disobedient characters who seek knowledge (and its concomitant, power) ceaselessly captivate the human, literary imagination. Despite the invectives against the first knowledge-seeker, indeed, the praise for the quest and for the necessary disobedience often finds eloquent affirmation. This affirmation might indicate that the will to ethical self-domination, to ethical self-rule, springs quite as eternally as proverbial hope. And this at no small cost.

Consider, for example, a perennial favorite among the outcast and disobedient, Lucifer. Humans might identify with this figure for no more complex a reason than that he, too, suffered eviction. Certainly Baudelaire's infamous *Litanies to Satan* dare proclaim kinship. Baudelaire addresses the "Prince of Exiles" as ally, mentor, and an example not entirely negative:

> Adopted father of those whom God
> the Father
> In his fury has driven from the
> earthly paradise
> Satan, have mercy on my endless
> suffering.

Nor is Baudelaire's fascination with Satan without literary precedent.

So marked is Milton's fascination with Lucifer that critics in literary and religious circles alike debate whether his portrait of the Evil One is not, ultimately, more attractive than that of the Good One. But, oddly enough, Milton's treatment of Lucifer differs from his treatment of Eve, although both these mythic characters are outcasts, exiles, iconoclasts.

Oddly, I say, because informative and vigorous debate does not surround Milton's portrait of the first human to disobey, to taste the forbidden fruit. Milton's Eve is vain, petulant, addlepated. One might attribute this one-dimensionality to the historical moment, of course. That is, Milton composed his bleak condemnation (and brilliant poetics) during a time of political and spiritual upheaval.

Therefore, as a Puritan and a servant of the state, Milton desired to translate those harsh, Pauline proscriptions against sexual pleasure and Cavalier delights into rhythmic, authoritative pentameter. Second, the Interregnum society needed a timely reminder that woman's role was "to rule by obedience and by submission sway." The routing of Charles I and the shattered doctrine of divine right of kings altered the entire idea of hierarchical order. What if, in turn, women no longer accepted the slightly idolatrous suggestion that they serve God through men? What if women sought to serve directly?

To encourage both stasis and change, possibly, Milton's grievous portrait of the first mother, the first (or second)* woman, the first seeker of knowledge seemed, socially and religiously, both necessary and useful. But of course, Milton's expressed desire to explain the ways of God to man seems, from our twentieth-century vantage point, blackly humorous. His dictating such weighty polemics to his daughter might be excused, then, as a blind necessity.

But that Eve's errant willfulness should be castigated in contemporary times and literary criticism seems unsettling. Consider, for example, how these pervasive assumptions of sexual shame, male supremacy, and Eve's unmitigated evil influence even so insightful a critic as Northrop Frye. Because of my personal pleasure in reading Frye, his rather flat and un-imaginative analysis of Milton's Eve seems the more disappoint-ing. Since Frye pursues seriously the mythic and romantic threads which weave together literature and religion, I was most interested in how he might, from his perspective as a modern, fairly enlightened man, review Milton's assumptions about male dominance and female subordination.** Frye's interpretation, while—as always—engaging stylistically, fails to note any im-balance in Milton's fascination for Lucifer's disobedience and

---

* According to *Myth & Legends of Ancient Israel,* Lilith and Adam enjoyed simultaneous creation; Lilith refused obedience to Adam and, by speaking the secret name of God, 'escaped' from Eden. I am men-tioning this, aware that Lilith's influence on female identification has been refuted by classifying her as either demon or fallen angel. That scholars, Biblical scholars, debate the androgynous Godhead intimated by the discrepancies between the first and second versions of human creation is important because a reexamination of sexual equality must follow. The current Pope, John-Paul II, is introducing Jungian concepts into the interpretations of Gensis, indeed, which may have intriguing ramifications for the Roman Catholic Church. To some Biblical scholars, as Fr. Andrew Greeley ironically remarks, "It almost sounds as if he were deliberately propounding feminist propaganda about androgyny." *North Country Catholic,* Jan. 9, 1980, p. 6.

** It may prove significant that Frye is an ordained minister of the United Church of Canada.

condemnation of Eve's.

To be precise, Frye accepts without difficulty Milton's contention that Eve's apple nourishes only carnal knowledge and that even that knowledge is—in Eve's hands—evil. In Frye's series of lectures on Milton's epics, *Return of Eden*, Eve seems the least complex character:

> As soon as Eve has eaten of the apple she becomes jealous
> of Adam, that is, her love for Adam is immediately
> perverted into jealousy and jealousy is essentially a
> feeling of possessiveness.[1]

This first assumption, that Eve's knowledge of good and evil is reduced to an emotional petulance, seems disturbing. But his reader still willingly assumes that Frye will contest, at some point, Milton's fundamental (pun intended) premise.

Yet Frye's twentieth-century insights only reinforce Milton's assumptions, unquestioningly. To Frye, as to Milton, the female with knowledge can do only evil:

> The supremacy of Adam over Eve is the free and human
> relation; the supremacy of Eve could soon become a road
> leading to intellectual enslavement.[2]

The female is assumed, when in a leadership position, an "enslaving" force; conversely, Adam's rule is deemed both ordained and "free."

Why does no other interpretation of this action and its principal players occur to a critic of Frye's considerable imagination? So pervasive are assumptions about Eve and "curious" females (and subsequent, punitive male supremacy over her access to knowledge of good and evil) that our most insightful critics are often blind to these assumptions. In a revivifying, necessary re-analysis of Milton's thought and historical perspective, Milton's poetic achievement need not be contested, of course.

But what should be contested is this accepted, Manichaean doctrine of sexuality in which the female signifies the evil force, the male the good. As Simone deBeauvoir rather persuasively argues, establishing the male as One and the female as Other prevents equality, socially or spiritually, as institutions exist.

That is, religious and social law (which, as Marx and Engels remind us, are bicameral legislators of the status quo) define the female as auxiliary to the male. This grows from, as deBeauvoir contends, the castigation of Eve which places "her daughters in a very bad position; everyone knows how severely the fathers of the church berated women."[3] In the reproving words of that famous church father, John Chrysostom: "The woman taught once, and ruined all. On this account . . . let her not teach. The whole female race transgressed."

The whole female race: in the relationship with knowledge of good and evil, Chrysostom considers females not only second class heavenly citizens. He considers women a race apart; this dictum inspired neither anger nor ridicule. John Chrysostom was canonized for insisting that no female should seek ethical self-rule, for that is precisely what "knowledge of good and evil" demands. To have half the race (human and collective) inured against decision-making, especially regarding ethics, seems a perilous and disturbing dogma.

The concept of the will-less woman, advanced under the banner of the Virgin Mary figure, counters this idea of the willful, fallen female: Eve. The dichotomy only *seems* to distinguish between one kind of female and another; the essential prohibition against the female's asserting her will, obtaining knowledge, and identifying herself as an ethically responsible human remains firm.* Discontent with this unholy paradox seems resurgent; our time is particularly a time of religious reappraisals. Analyses of the socio-spiritual confinement of female identity abound; consider Mary Daly's *Beyond God the Father* and Merlin Stone's *When God Was A Woman* and Sarah Pomeroy's *Goddesses, Whores, Wives and Slaves* and J. Edgar Bruns' *God As Woman, Woman as God,* and, a classic work from the turn of the century, Elizabeth Cady Stanton's *The Woman's Bible.*

An exerpt from Bruns' book, tracing Pandora/Eve/Ianna, indicates the fundamental problem with the Judeo-Christian castigation of the female's relationship with knowledge. Eve, the knowledge-giver, is no longer treated as Athena, the knowledge-giver. Bruns notes "a gradual inversion of the role of wo-

---

* "If knowledge is power, power is also knowledge, and a factor in their subordinate position is the fairly systematic ignorance patriarchy imposes upon women." Kate Millett, *Sexual Politics,* p. 66.

man" throughout the patriarchal reinterpretations of myth until, presently, the female "is no longer associated with knowledge but altogether with misfortune."[4]

Ethical self-rule is forbidden fruit; the female, as adjured by St. Clement of Alexandria, must not contemplate her nature because it is through her nature that humanity suffered its fall.* Thus, the very act of acquiring self-knowledge, the first act of the heroic personality, is prohibited to woman. Little wonder that, given such socio-spiritual imperatives against knowledge of self, Alexander Pope smugly announces, in a delightful couplet of deleterious intent:**

> Nothing so true as what you once let fall,
> "Most women have no Characters at all."

*

Abuses of Enchantment

Not only in the great religious allegory of Eve (Life) and Adam (Dust) are females and males adjured to distrust the female's choice of knowledge. Even in fairyland, the "curious" female is punished; even the daughters of atheists, alas, cannot evade this insidious instruction. As popularly interpreted, sacred and secular tales socialize children into their proper roles: male, active and female, passive.

Thus, in the most popular and repeated tales, the heroine *is* rescued, *is* awakened; she blissfully rests in the passive voice, in

---

* While the literature regarding this theological issue is enormous, I recommend that those intrigued by the issues read Mary Daly or, failing that, obtain a quick, insightful survey of the literature by reading "Theologian: The New Heretics" by Tom F. Driver in the April 6, 1980 *Book Review* section of the New York *Times*.

** This couplet from "Epistle II: To a Lady: Of the Characters of Women" is included among Pope's Moral Essays, interestingly enough; his speaker ascribes this deadly line to a woman, a woman whom he intends to elevate, as any woman might expect, into the usual "extraordinary" woman.

what Kay Stone calls a passive state of "arrested development" as Sleeping Beauty. The bifurcation follows the usual sexual lines. "Heroes succeed because they act, not because they are. They are judged not by their appearance or inherent sweet nature but by their ability to overcome obstacles. . . ."[5] While Bettelheim feels sure, in his analysis of such tales, that "there are probably tales where the courage and determination of females rescue males,"[6] he does not analyze any of them. His *Uses of Enchantment*, although a restrictively Freudian study of fairytales, does indicate how myths and secular stories cross-pollinate to advance similar, gender-related morals.

That social stories and religious parables are mainstays of social identification hardly constitutes a wildly new theory, of course. The widely read and influential psychiatrist, Eric Berne, too, feels "that fairytales offer not only dreams and hopes but actual programs for behavior."[7] And the notable Joseph Campbell asserts that sacred and profane tales are "essentially tutorial." Campbell is mindful, too, that the line separating the sacred from the secular story is a penumbral one indeed.

In his commentary on a Pantheon edition of the Grimms' collected tales, in fact, Campbell places all these tales under the umbrella term, myth. His assertion that "Myth is psychology misread as cosmology, history, and biography"[8] would surely please such Freudians as Erik Erikson and Bruno Bettelheim. And if such is the case, tales can *imbue* neurosis as well as trace it; the almost pathologically passive female and the almost megalomaniacally active male find, perhaps, their origins in these approved texts.

Unquestionably, sacred and secular tales ordain the rule of the male over the female. When, for example, the female takes the initiative, seeks adventure, displays curiosity, she is penalized. Cursed by a supernatural being for her disobedience, the female in fairyland falls into sleep or exile (Sleeping Beauty/Rapunzel) and can be awakened/redeemed only through—predictably enough—the curiosity and willfulness of a male/prince.

And repeatedly, as Bettleheim indicates, "the female is strongly tempted to do what is forbidden her."[9] What is forbidden her is to know: what lies behind the door, within the chest, under the lamp? Whether Sleeping Beauty or Psyche, her quest for knowledge is defined as a disobedient act. Willful seeking places her in such difficult straits that only the willful, custodial male can rescue her.

And yet this is but one of several paradoxical lessons. These psychologists and anthropologists insist that maturity demands knowledge of good and evil. Indeed, ethical self-determination depends upon disobedience and initiative. That a female (princess or archetype) should aspire to self-rule is, however, not condoned. In discussing innocence and experience, these authorities (Bettelheim, Erikson, Berne, Campbell) lack Blake's vision; they affirm, however, the loss of Eden and parental (mortal or divine) approbation.

As Bettelheim argues, to remain obediently in a metaphorical Eden "where nothing is demanded of him and all of his desires are met as soon as he expresses them" threatens to become more than "empty and boring."[10] Such stasis, finally, proves enervating. In this analysis, of course, Bettelheim employs a basic Freudian assumption of infantile paradise and the adult's return through memory and death.* Disobedience and exile are, indeed, prerequisites for maturation.

> . . . each child in his development must repeat the history of man, real or imagined. We are all expelled from the original paradise of infancy.[11]

In order to develop "a separate self," to gain "initiative and self-determination," and to discern "the difference between good and evil," the individual must dare to provoke the displeasure of the powers that be, must, indeed, relinquish a status quo paradise. What remains problematic is the continued castigation of the female for taking necessary action, for becoming an ethical being. As Marie-Louise von Franz summarizes in *Problems of the Feminine in Fairytales:*

> We are still confronted with the paradox that it is a sin to become conscious and a sin to remain unconscious.[12]

---

* Mircea Eliade's *Myth and Reality* discusses this nexus in an engaging, informed manner.

Yet, more often than not, literature seems to celebrate the sinful pursuit of knowledge of good and evil, despite mythic and fairytale proscriptions against such a disobedient act. Judiciously at times, literature celebrates the quest for a metaphorical, inviolable Eden created by an individual, eked out from a desperately won exile. Such works posit that the refusal to obey or observe the conventional restrictions revivifies, in fact, the quest for knowledge.

Philosophically this impulse finds translation even in contemporary thought. Surely the craze for individuated ethics, "Situation Ethics," comes to mind. More enduringly, perhaps, Paul Tillich's popular, influential tract, *The Courage to Be* promotes this drive toward self-determination as a basic, ethical imperative:

> . . . in commanding itself becomes its own judge and
> its own victim . . . in doing this the courageous self
> is united with life itself and its secrets.[13]

Likewise, this attitude toward disobedience as an ethical imperative and toward knowledge of good and evil as a necessary quest finds eloquent defense in the writings of Soren Kierkegaard. His "fear and trembling" stipulates belief in personal *conscience:* acting with knowledge. Apparently, seeking knowledge of good and evil can promote ethical disobedience. The breaking of existing laws of conduct can occur through recognizing an other, equally ethical necessity.

Nor do philosophy and literature examine such disobedient acts, such disobedient actors, only as allegorical or archetypal characters. The common man and, as should become apparent, the common woman who seek responsibility for and knowledge of good and evil are also celebrated. Thus, utterly human characters like Stephen Daedalus of James Joyce's *A Portrait of the Artist as a Young Man* manifest this same urge to risk knowledge, this same self-assurance.

With his famous, decisive "non-serviam,"* Stephen chooses physical and metaphysical exile, although he cannot delineate its full and lasting consequences. Nevertheless, he leaves not

---

* "I will not serve."

only family and homeland but also custom, politics, religion, former identifiers. He determines—and this seems the quintessential human act—to direct his own destiny.

Like his archetypal mother, such a hero determines for himself issues of good and evil. As Adrienne Rich notes, such acts are forbidden Biblically and socially: "Every act of becoming conscious / it says here in this book) / is an unnatural act."[14] Some disobey. Yet the way to such commitment, to such knowledge is arduous, blocked. The literature of human experience agrees that the way out of fairyland/Eden and into the quest is forboding. Even in fairyland, after all, the path is blocked by supernatural powers or dragons or murderous briars. But the desire for "knowledge of good and evil"—even when that desire is an amorphous, barely articulated desire—is primordial.

Highly articulate men and women repeatedly express this desire for the responsibilities of self-rule. From Margaret Fuller, as from James Joyce, the essential recognition is the same: social and religious definitions not only discourage self-goverance but actively oppose it. While Joyce's manifesto is lauded and understandably so, Margaret Fuller's eloquent summary of this human problem in its female aspect is only recently receiving a hearing:

> What Woman needs is not as a woman to act or rule, but
> as nature to grow, as an intellect to discern, as a soul to
> live freely and unimpeded, to unfold such powers as were
> given her when we left our common home.[15]

When Freud issued his sincere and plaintiff cry regarding what women want, this nation seems not to have answered the question with Fuller's ample and exact statement. That Fuller chooses this metaphor of mutual exile is intriguing not only because of its obvious connection with our first encounter with knowledge but also because exile is a necessary condition of transcendence for Joyce, as well.

To gain self-knowledge—for where else does knowledge of good and evil begin—requires moving beyond, potentially, the "good" and "evil" defined by existing orders: the church and the state. And so Stephen Daedalus suspects—as do many knowledgeable exiles—that the ruling powers concoct notions of crime and sin, of insanity and heresy to maintain the status quo.　Such seekers suspect, too, that no Authority can know for them, and the State, even the family, can curtail rather than protect and advance human knowledge of good and evil.

Literature, apparently, refuses to assume what some religious and social institutions rather summarily assume: that this impulse toward self-determination is *necessarily* evil.　To many heroes/heroines in literature, apparently, obedience seems slavish; convention masks or can mask a deadening conformity which *seems* to be order.　In fine, literature often celebrates the sinner, the iconoclast, the exile.

Moreover, literature sometimes extols the notion that the obedient accomplish the goals of others, while the disobedient establish their own goals.　In this, creative writing seems to refute that Judeo-Christian supposition that disobedience and the quest for knowledge for good and evil (which are causally linked) are negative.　But while reviewing such physically or metaphysically exiled characters as Hesse's Emil Sinclair and Hemingway's Jake Barnes and Joyce's Richard Rowan, I suddenly noticed a dearth of women.

Where might those disobedient females be?　I decided to examine some literature by and about females in order to note how females rebel against sacred and secular identities.　Social and religious institutions which, according to such venerable writers as Joyce and Hesse, oppress the male individual in his quest for knowledge of good and evil might reasonably be supposed to exert equal pressure against the female quester.

That women in myth and fable have an enduring—albeit damaged—reputation for desiring "forbidden fruit" helped assure me that the daughters of Eve must be active in the land. What might her fictional/factual daughters (the characters/the authors) seek?　risk?　discover?　Eve, the first human to disobey and to obtain "knowledge of good and evil" shared that knowledge (and its ethical implications); she considered it, perhaps as she was told, a godly prerogative for which a high price should be exacted.

What is the going rate for such knowledge?　What devices do authors use to indicate both the proscriptions against "curious" females and the undeniable desire for such self-rule: the forbidden fruit?

Romance: Ironic Modification

In her fine collection of literary criticism and personal reminiscence, *The Eye of the Story,* Eudora Welty includes a lecture presented to the eminent Mississippi Historical Society. The lecture indicates precisely how myths and secular stories serve the purposes of a particular writer. Welty calls this technique "ironic modification" and discusses its uses in "Fairy Tale of the Natchez Trace," her lecture.

Welty explains how the famous fairytale and her second novel, *The Robber Bridegroom,* are aligned through her uses of "ironic modification." Welty asserts that "it was by no accident that I made our local history and the legend and the fairytale into working equivalents in the story I came to write."[16] Set in a particular region and historical moment, Welty's novel attains a timeless force through the use of folklore motifs, characterization, and usual expectation.

The Robber Bridegroom is deeply concerned with issues of identity and knowledge of good and evil; the novel is, in turn, deeply concerned with issues of love and responsibility. The protagonists, Rosamund and Jamie, are at once quotidian and archetypal; they seem part fairytale, part myth, part commonplace Mississippi. Rosamund's crisis involves discovering Jamie's "true face," his true identity. She makes, as Welty puts it, "her version of the classic mistake."[17] Jamie plays Cupid to Rosamund's Psyche.

Welty uses these parallel notions of mythic mistakes and fairytale lovers not, however, to reinforce the foolishness of Psyche/Rosamund. Rather, she affirms the necessity of knowledge and its concomitant responsibilities. To seek knowledge of Jamie's true identity is, of course, forbidden; Rosamund's sense of ethical identity provokes her into risking disobedience and loss. This method of altering either components or moral lessons of such sacred/secular tales is Welty's "ironic modification."

While Welty names the technique, it is hardly foreign to the literary tradition and vocabulary. "Ironic modification" can serve as a fully developed structural element, as in B. J. Chute's *A Fairytale* and Selma Lagerlof's *The Treasure* or as a brief, vastly informing allusion as in Joyce Carol Oates' *Do*

With Me What You Will.* Each novel in this analysis, of course, employs "ironic modification."

That such "ironic modification" indicates the invisible/ visible links between sacred and secular socialization anchors the writer, as well, to the romantic tradition of literature. Yoked together by Judeo-Christian myths, females and males have translated the mutual burden of a punitive exile into a somewhat lovelier illusion while strictly maintaining the division placed between the sexes. This translation is simple: from the curse of male labor comes the myth of material joy; from the curse of female labor arises the myth of sustaining love.

Money marries love; becoming mates with being; prince and princess mate. Of course, the romantic illusion is realized only between the covers of a much-maligned, best-selling Barbara Cartland novel. Only there is the hero able to protect and provide, the heroine able to nurture and cherish. As Anne Sexton quite summarily puts it: "And thus they were married/ and lived together on a sugarcube."[18] Material need, demanding children, the will to change: none of this mars the perfect stasis created by the perfect couple. In proper time, faultlessly polite children and ample funds appear like beatific proofs of their romantic perfection.

And while nobody professes belief in it anymore, this romantic illusion finds reflection even in our most thoughtful, artistic, enduring literature. The presentation differs predictably from that in the gossamer romance and fairytale genres. But the essential desire to make the curses into cure-alls, to make the dangerous links between females and males seem romantically destined, remains a haunting desire. Thus, while adults assiduously refute identification with princess and prince, the expectation lingers that "happily ever after" is an emotional/ material Eden which two can reenter.

Despite this longing for redemption through love and ease in exile through money, writers concede that romance is often more pose than position. It is as much illusion as emotion, and, indeed, the ego seems often so enthralled with gestures of loving

---

* This refrain from the fairytale, "The Maiden Without Hands," underscores the physical and emotional violence so characteristic of Oates' opus.

that the act itself seems a disappointment. Nor is this
fundamental disappointment a female one. Thus, Jimmy Gatz
is obsessed with becoming a prince that he may win the
princess; he objectifies the beloved into a dangerous ideal.
The real Daisy Buchanan—a vapid, immoral embodiment of
the pretty princess—deserves little attention and less approval.
In Fitzgerald's *The Great Gatsby*, as in Chopin's *The Awakening*,
the notion, universally approved, that love is blind is not the
only stock, romantic notion receiving a second glance.

The male/female roles and expectations translated into
a romantic position remain stultifying; the dream linking the
gold to the golden girl destroys the female ethically and the
male physically. Thus the romantic notion of passive princess/
active prince is not merely puerile; it is fatal. Nostalgia for
this dream works inside this novel which exposes it: *The Great
Gatsby* for example, loves and hates the illusion.

Often proclaimed one of that ever-resurgent breed, "the
last of the Romantics," Fitzgerald employs romantic elements
to expose the poverty of the illusion: pretty people, lavish
settings, "pink cocktail music,"* privileges. Yet in these novels,
the romantic illusion becomes a beast with teeth, and those
teeth are usually buried in the neck of a romantically victimized
male. This hero, a prototype from myth and fairyland, quests
gold and the golden girl as he might the Grail; in *Tender Is the
Night*, as in *Gatsby*, this dual obsession is lethal. The princess
is a killer; Nicole attains her mental health at the expense of
Dick Diver's; Daisy avoids responsibility for killing Myrtle
Wilson through Jay Gatsby's unethical sacrifice.

Gatsby sees Daisy "in a white palace the king's daughter,"
the golden girl.[19] To gain prince and castle, however, Daisy
chooses Tom Buchanan. These two, degenerate and immoral
people, embody the love and money illusion. They destroy
with impunity; long before the proletariate fiction of the '30's

---

* In *The Great Gatsby: a Facsimile of the Manuscript* in Fitzgerald's
own hand, edited by Matthew J. Bruccoli and put out by Washington, D.
C.'s Microcard Edition Books in 1973, the cocktail music is "yellow" and,
interestingly enough, one of the key activities described by Fitzgerald is
the use of narcotics, of "dope" at this, Gatsby's party.

and the highly self-conscious Watergate generation, Fitzgerald exposes white collar/white skirt crime as a prerogative of the rich. Different legal systems exist for different classes. Or, to put it more romantically, to represent the romantic illusion (love and money) is to enjoy freedom from moral/legal responsibilities.*

Thus, in the novels of F. Scott Fitzgerald, "ironic modification" almost completely inverts the female/male socialization. It is not merely the double standard which breeds irresponsible creatures of privilege but the whole romantic illusion of how males and females define themselves and interact. In Fitzgerald, the material well-being which indicates "election" confuses the spiritual life. The Lord's love seems to follow the wealthy American male as surely as the love of a princess does. This whole sordid notion finds its "ironic modification" in this putatively romantic writer.

And Fitzgerald's sensitivity to the horrors of these fairy-tale identities is grounded in astute observation of the privileged. Yet, even as they recognize the inanity and peril of this dual dream of love/money—the transvaluation of the curses of Genesis—writers find it hard to dismiss the identities and expectations set by sacred and secular tales. This seems transparently obvious in works by John O'Hara and John Cheever, for example. Thus O'Hara's males represent the sad waste of keeping appointments in Samarra, need, of escaping the ennui and mechanization of "the good life" through suicide, through alcohol. And their wives seem devitalizing and devitalized.

Similarly, and replete with images from romantic lore, John Cheever's protagonists remember the golden ways and the golden girls of Princeton days and the promises of wealth and of love. Cheever's commuters reflect on these dreams, staring into railroad car windows, then step into waiting station-wagons and arrive promptly home to the predictably dry martini. The American, white male seems consumed by love and money as realized in the romantic tradition. Yet we remain

---

* Walter Sutton, Harrison T. Meserole, and Brom Weber, editors of *American Literature* (Lexington, D. C. Heath, 1969) consider *Gatsby* "an indictment of American capitalistic culture as powerful as any set forth in the proletarian fiction . . ." of the subsequent generations.

more likely to criticize the dreamer than the dream. And when anti-Romantics, Norman Mailer, for example, describe *An American Dream*, America is dying of cancer and rifle wounds; his domestic novels employ a war-zone value system and his characters must do without not just the illusion of love but love itself. Little hope here to return to Eden.

Nor is "ironic modification" the tool solely of novelists, of course. Exposure to such expectations and identities (as curious female/redeeming male; as princess/prince) are guaranteed by both sacred and secular stories. Nevertheless, poets seem as dedicated as prose writers to refuting these identity patterns. A recent example of such "ironic modification" is the award-winning volume by Olga Broumas, *Beginning with O.*

Two sections of this three-part volume recreate sacred tales ("Twelve Aspects of God") and secular stories ("Innocence"). Broumas surely alters common expectations; her "Cinderella," for example, refuses to be a princess: "A woman co-opted by promises."[20] Cinderella refuses, moreover, to remain isolated and powerless "in a house of men/who secretly/call themselves princes." And this Aschenputtel even issues a command, a highly irregular practice among fairytale females; the imperative constitutes yet another "ironic modification" since prince, castle, riches are all foresworn: "Give/me my ashes. A cold stove, a cinderblock pillow, wet/ canvas shoes in my sisters'/, my sisters' hut. Or I swear/I'll die young/like those favored before me, hand-picked each one/for her joyful heart."

For both prince and princess, then, the romantic ideal promises little but imprisonment, stasis, death. Broumas's goddesses and princesses redefine themselves and, often, awaken one another from the romantic illusion. In Broumas's "ironic modification" of the Sleeping Beauty, for example, the dormant female is awakened by rather unexpected royalty: "I/wake to your public kiss. Your name/is Judith." Certainly, Sapphic implications guide Broumas's "ironic modification" of many tales, characters, and morales.

But heterosexual implications do guide another justly famous volume: *Transformations.* In this lusty, ascerbic collection, Anne Sexton retells the most popular and romantic of our fairytales. Her tone and intentions are ironic indeed; Sexton attains through "the surprise of juxtaposition" essential

"similes that deflate romance, humor as black as ebony."[21]
Sexton, through imagery and a highly caustic narrative voice,
achieves "ironic modification." This narrator stresses the basic
and distressing differences between romantic expectation and
actual, emotional experience.

Note, for example, the "ironic modification" regarding
the conclusion of the revered tale, "Cinderella":

> Lived, they say, happily ever after,
> like two dolls in a museum case
> never bothered by diapers or dust
> never arguing over the timing of an egg,
> never telling the same story twice,
> never getting a middle-aged spread,
> their darling smiles painted on for eternity,
> Regular Bobbsey Twins.
> That story.[22]

Given ironic modification of both point of view and imagery,
"happily ever after" signifies entropy; the emotional goal seems
a penal one. The promise of transforming kisses is a half-truth;
Sexton chastizes promoters of such romantic fancies as being
either fools or hypocrites yet counts herself among this
company.

A self-proclaimed addict to such tales, Sexton admits to
weaning herself incompletely, and with great difficulty, from
identities of princess and prince.* Although, throughout *Transformations,* Sexton "undermines the fairy tale with deadly
address and merciless employment of the city-American
idiom,"[23] her persona seems shaken by such basic irony as that
inherent in the tales themselves. In her retellings, the romantic
illusion leaves prince/princess transformed in sinister ways;
they live in a box "painted identically blue," and the marriage
bed—given Sexton's relentless "ironic modification"—becomes
"a kind of coffin/a kind of blue funk./Is it not?"[24]

This is a deadly assessment; Sexton's equation of love
and death has about it none of the perilous ecstasy reminiscent

---

* In an interview at SUNY Brockport, Sexton declared herself "obsessed" by such stories through her 'teens.'

of John Donne. Indeed, this entire collection might most please
the Freudians who seem still oddly happy when love is fatal
and the artist neurotic. So sophisticated is the tone throughout
this volume and so arresting the "ironic modification" that
Sexton's prose-poems inspire agitation. The battle of the sexes
seems a war of vicious misunderstanding and infantile expectation. To believe the romantic myth is mad; to dispose of it
seems as difficult as flaying oneself alive.

In adult poems and novels, "ironic modification" seems
a necessary tool, a lens, perhaps, with which to refocus human
emotions and identities and expectations. Such "ironic modification" seems, finally, an act of sheer survival; exiled from
both sacred and secular illusions, adults seem "stunned at the
suddenly/possible shifts of meaning for which/like amnesiacs/in
a ward on fire, we must/find words/or burn."[25] "Ironic modification" seems, then, a mode through which writers examine
knowledge of good and evil, the ethical equations of folk and
sacred stories, and their hold upon the human imagination.

In the novels examined in this work, "ironic modification"
helps provide the words which allow the protagonists to escape
rather than be consumed by knowledge. Since "the popularized
heroines of Grimms and Disney are not only passive and pretty,
but also unusually patient, obedient, industrious, and quiet,"[26]
a predictable "ironic modification" might include the creation
of a heroine who inverts one or all of these princess-prerequisites.

And such is, indeed, the case. Atwood's surfacer, for
example, is more taciturn than quiet. And she alone has knowledge of the wilderness; she controls the lives of two men and
another woman on an isolated island. Illustrating a book of
fairytales and being in this oracular place bring the protagonist
into knowledge of identities beyond that of obedient woman
and aging princess.

In Doris Lessing's *The Summer Before the Dark,* the heroine
realizes her personal connection with the romantic illusion, her
self-deception in perpetuating its forms and roles. She, too,
examines fairytale identities and expectations and attains a
difficult passage into knowledge of good and evil as this knowledge influences selfhood. Likewise, Kate Chopin's "ironic
modification" allows Edna Pontellier insight; the protagonist
awakens herself from the metaphorical sleep of the romantic
illusion.

Selma Lagerlöf's *The Treasure* employs the ancient language of the fairytale as an "ironic modification." The promise of prince and castle is not considered an evil promise; nevertheless, deeper and higher actions may be demanded of an erstwhile princess who must be—first and foremost—an ethical woman. Thus, choosing the prince and the correlative earthly delights can, according to "ironic modifications" in *The Treasure*, be an escape from responsibility. Lagerlöf's heroine meets the ultimate demands of knowledge of good and evil; Elsalill elects to make Antigone's choice rather than Cinderella's, if indeed one ever thinks of Cinderella as making a choice.

From Welty to Broumas to Fitzgerald, writers examine identity through conventional sacred and secular models. Certainly these writers are familiar with the fusion of sin and sexuality extolled in the Old Testament and reinforced by Pauline injunctions in the New. Romance and punishment are linked, even if the curses of Genesis *seem* to be transformed as magically as coach mice. That the romantic illusion might be limiting invites, indeed, "ironic modification."

> We had to take the world as it was given
> The nursemaid sitting passive in the park
> Was rarely by a changeling prince accosted.

"IDEAL LANDSCAPE"
Adrienne Rich

*

Feminist Perspective

In attempting to explicate what seems already transparently obvious—that my critical perspective is a feminist one—I am reminded of a finer writer's assessment of this dilemma, this having to provide extensive exegesis of the obvious.

ME: My internist has asked me to cut down gradually on my consumption of statistics about American women.

I: Why?

> ME: It's sort of sad. Say I read that only nineteen
>   American women became orthodontists in 1962.
>   I am humiliated, depressed. I cry easily. It's
>   days before I think to be glad that so few *wanted*
>   to be orthodontists, do you see?[27]

By thus prefacing her *Thinking About Women* (1969), Mary Ellmann establishes a tone no more world-weary than amused, no less ardently feminist than wittily individual. Volition and oppression exist side by side; there is both progress and stasis. Ellmann's lively criticism reminds us that the reader's movement of the women's movement has a sense of humor and a sense of the grotesque, as well. Her writing is precise, self-assured, and unabashedly argumentative.

The mind of Mary Ellmann is thinking about women, and that mind is trained in literature. What she opines about the state of the art has proved worthy of animated debate among people interested in writing—be they feminists or masculinists or self-proclaimed hermaphroditists. Ellmann's remarks on Austen or Mailer or Plath or Lessing or Joyce are (while assuredly not Richard's, who can also think) engaging and interesting. She recognizes the impropriety of slavish sexual analogy applied to anything, literature included.

But the world—including this literary one—has long been bifurcated along sexual lines. Mary Ellmann notes Robert Lowell's obvious discomfort in his introduction to the now famous volume, *Ariel* by Sylvia Plath. To certify to the poet's vast talents *and* gender, Robert Lowell stamps the work and its author "girlish," then "hardly a person at all," then barely "a women," and—as a compliment—"certainly not another poetess," and so on until the conflagration over Plath's being a female poet seems to obscure the heat and light of the poems themselves.

Ellmann reasons that if such a preeminent person as Robert Lowell encountered such distress—and words were his very business—then some thinking about how we think about women is, indeed, in order. In order to make such peregrination as simple as possible, I shall endeavor, therefore, to define terms. Words need hardly seem the choice of weapons aimed at any particularly devilish advocate. So I offer this necessary angel: at last, the definitive definition of that shifty word, that nemesis of lexicographers and linguists alike: feminist.

Feminist:

This is a fractious word indeed; "feminist" is both adjective and noun, both person and position. It is, denotatively and connotatively, what used to be called a "fightin' word." It is as contrary, as elusive as its partner and adversary, "masculinist."

What the "masculinist" position is and who might best represent it seems as shifty an issue as its sister issue. Norman Mailer is "masculinist" but not as John Cheever is; John Updike is "masculinist" but not as James Dickey is. And that the "masculinist" assumes other identifying terms simultaneously seems to both confuse and clarify the issue. Thus, for example, Hesse is decidedly "masculinist" but also a patented "humanist."

In turn, a "feminist" may also be a Socialist or a Daughter of the American Revolution: consider Emma Goldman, consider Eleanor Roosevelt. (Whether, of course, *any* Young Republican ever has or ever will be a self-affirmed "feminist" may prove more than a semantical question.)

But I do not mean to beg the question merely by obfuscating it: feminist. Since any work dealing primarily with works written by women is usually tagged "feminist" (and that exclusively), some further clarification seems still in order. And so: "feminist" is the person who continually finds the self in the arduous process of defining feminist/female/feminine/Woman/women and—in turn—masculinist/male/masculine/Man/men. Within the category stands a crowd, granted; representatives engaged in this pursuit are as disparate as Phyllis Schlafly and Kate Millett and John Irving.

So can it be that a feminist might also be a male person continually finding himself in the process of defining feminist/female/Woman/women and—in turn—etcetera? Surely, whether a male can indeed *be* a feminist (whether Jesus was one remains a subject of much lively, spurious debate) remains before the court. John Stuart Mill rather eloquently presents—as does Henrik Ibsen—the case for the male-feminist.

"Male-feminist," the "female-masculinist," note how these gender-identifiers begin to multiply like some Malthusian nightmare or—to keep the analogy sexual—like guppies, rabbits, sparrows. To define "feminist" and never be called upon to define "masculinist" seems, to use an old-fashioned, out-of-favor word, "sexist." To define "feminist" or "masculinist" threatens to be, if not merely one-dimensional, both myopic and inane. So Mary Ellmann is undoubtedly correct in deeming the whole gender-literary-identification business part tedium, part necessity.

The incessant speechifying about the superiority (always natural or ordained) of one genital system over an "other," as it were, reaches the point of diminishing returns. The question of good literature threatens to be obscured by its secondary sexual characteristics. (There are—even in Academe—males who will not read literature by women; women who will not read literature by men do not, usually, find themselves long in Academe.)

"It is unpleasant," Ellmann quietly reminds us, "to be *obliged* to divide the contents of the universe into two categories of male and female."[28]   Nor is this exasperation with obsessive, required gender-identified classification new.   Provoked by pointless discriminations about "the feminine hand" and "the feminine foot" during the ardently feminist 1890's, Charlotte Perkins Gilman offered the following timely, anatomical reminder: "A hand is an organ of prehension; a foot is an organ of locomotion; they are not secondary sexual characteristics."[29]

No more is literary style and achievement; thus, the same might be said of literature but, until a good deal more "thinking about women" and subsequent "thinking about men" has been accomplished, it probably won't be.   And this sustained fascination with sexuality qua literary achievement may prove a passing, puerile, Freudian idee fixe. Perhaps we shall outgrow it, "feminists" and "masculinists" alike.   Or—more likely—the sexual critical perspectives will simply become an assumed, valuable component of the critical tradition like Marxist theory, like Freudian criticism.

Yet Feminist criticism—which began with the "Declaration of Sentiments" in 1848*—the same year in which Marx and Engels issued their *Communist Manifesto*—seems to find more difficulty in gaining acceptance. As is obvious to students of literature, however, such varied "isms" generate lively reconsiderations of any artist's works, of the ideas explored or ignored therein.   Marxist   revisionists   *read*   books   differently   than

---

* That is, the American Feminist Movement.

Freudian revisionists; this same difference distinguishes Feminist revisionists.

Such literary positions clarify parts of the literary whole previously obscured. What Arnold Kettle and various Marxist critics have added to the understanding of writers from Dickens to Lawrence typifies the rejuvenating effects of diverse critical positions. Edmund Wilson, in combining aspects of Humanism, Marxism and Freudian thought, produced a critical mode now commonly acclaimed as that of the "liberal imagination."

No movement or theory of critical revision occurs in vacuo; in no period of history is this tenet more obvious than in the tumultuous nineteenth-century. The revolotions of 1848, the *Communist Manifesto,* the voyage of the "Beagle," fill but a few years of that fateful and transforming time. But we are less familiar with Feminist proclamations which run parallel with these other, emancipating movements: the "Declaration of Sentiments" written in 1848, for example, and the great revisionist work of Elizabeth Cady Stanton and her Biblical scholars, *The Woman's Bible* (1895, 1898). The documents and ideas which present the female analysis of culture and of religion are, or have been, overlooked, making the female movements *seem* to exist in vacuo. And yet these divergent theories, from Engels to Veblen to Margaret Fuller, seem connected.

A veritable band-wagon of revolutionary theorists combined, each tooting cacophonous or harmonious point/ counter-points. Most of these theories had in common the supposition that religious and social institutions were limiting the possiblities of the individual and defining the sexes in a manner deleterious to social development. How the male/female experiences and identities were defined is fundamental to these revolutions in consciousness.

In "Origin of the Family, Private Property, and the State," (1886), for example, Frederich Engels remarks that "the first class oppression coincides with that of the female by the male."[30] This tenet of economic revolution—so oddly ignored in the political science and history classes of one's youth—attacks that much-praised Victorian unit: the family. The "natural supremacy" of Adam which Northrop Frye so comfortably accepts may, according to Frederich Engels, promote more knowledge of evil than knowledge of good.

Feminist criticism noted this destructive, economic, and

social division between the sexes, as is clear in the writings of Margaret Fuller and Lucretia Mott and John Stuart Mill and Elizabeth Cady Stanton.   About this time, too, Nietzsche expounded his lusty theories opposing all restraints against the individual; in no way, to my knowledge, can Nietzsche be considered a "feminist" because of his essential and proclaimed misogyny.   But what is interesting to note historically is that his declaring the Prime Mover of the social order dead seems more acceptable than Stanton's declaring Eve equal.   Thus, to attack male sovereignty seems, in light of history, more revolutionary than to attack the Deity.

Elizabeth Cady Stanton's *The Woman's Bible* (1895-1898) "shook many a true believer"[31] at a time when Noah's actual or allegorical ark was already tossing about on tumultuous seas of skepticism and social change.   Stanton and her Biblical scholars "boldly challenged the accepted theology at the same time other critics were re-examining the Bible in the new light of Darwinism."[32]   This major feminist work provides, indeed, the foundation for this study.   Stanton proclaims Eve's quest for the knowledge of good and evil a worthy one.

The roots for this entire book, indeed, seem struck by the feminist theories of one hundred years ago and more.   Yet to interpret this taking of the "forbidden fruit" a necessary gamble, even a laudable act, is a heresy more ancient than this one root implies.   The Pelagians of the fifth century, too, considered the notions of Original Sin and punitive exile untenable.

According to these heresies, the fundamental act of acquiring the knowledge of good and evil requires no prolonged curse upon our forebears.   That ethical action should ever be forbidden strikes the eminent Joseph Campbell of our own time as an odd, errant idea; in his readable *The Flight of the Wild Gander,* Campbell remembers a newsphoto flashed in the USA during World War II, showing two giant guardians before the gate of the Todaiji temple in Nara:

> . . . fierce figures with lifted swords. There was no picture
> of the temple itself, or of the Buddha within, beneath
> the Tree of Enlightenment, hand lifted in the 'fear-not'
> gesture, but only that one threatening cherub and be-

neath the picture the legend: "The Japanese worship
gods like this."*

Campbell reaches a conclusion little expected by the propa-
gandists at that time: "Not they, but we!" Campbell distinguishes the Asian idea of entering the gate, despite the guardians, and attaining the fruit of knowledge. "It is we," he notes,
"whose god would keep men (sic) out of the Garden."

Yet, despite these injunctions against seeking knowledge
of good and evil, humans seem unable to resist the quest.
Despite sanctions against woman's willful seeking of such "forbidden fruit," she persists. Confronted by the dragons (or armed
cherubs) of fairy tale and mythic guardians, the female protagonist somehow finds her way not only into the heart of the
Garden, but out of it.

The male—in his guise as God or prince—believes in his
dominion, in his ability to persuade the female (through punitive
or benevolent measures) that he alone must reign, that he alone
must be the keeper of the kingdom and the keeper of knowledge.
The daughters of Eve, however, risk disobedience and exile in
order to become ethically responsible not only for themselves
but for others.

From Selma Lagerlöf to Kate Chopin, from Margaret
Atwood to Doris Lessing, novelists still proclaim the quest for
knowledge of good and evil a lively, if forbidden, one. These
works insinuate, as did the Pelagian heretics and our Feminist
forebears, that we did not fall from the Garden. We leapt!

---

* This passage from *The Flight of the Wild Gander: Exploration in
the Mythological Imagination* (Chicago: Ragnery Company, 1972, p. 195)
provides wonderful insights into Campbell's peculiar and refreshing scrutiny
of detail so characteristic of his works.

Notes

[1] Northrop Frye, *Return of Eden* (Toronto: University of Toronto Press, 1965), p. 64.

[2] Frye, p. 65.

[3] Simon deBeauvoir, *The Second Sex,* trans. H. M. Parshley, (New York: Bantam Books, 1953), p. 210.

[4] J. Edgar Bruns, *God As Woman, Woman as God* (New York: Paulist Press, 1971), p. 22.

[5] Kay Stone, "Things Walt Disney Never Told Us," *Women and Folklore,* ed. Claire R. Farrer, (Austin: University of Texas Press, 1975), p. 48.

[6] Bruno Bettelheim, *The Uses of Enchantment* (New York: Vintage Press, 1977), p. 227.

[7] Stone, p. 58.

[8] Joseph Campbell, "Folkloristic Commentary, *The Complete Grimms' Fairy Tales,* (New York: Pantheon Books, 1949), p. 860.

[9] Bettelheim, p. 301.

[10] Bettelheim, p. 307.

[11] Bettelheim, p. 274.

[12] Marie-Louise von Franz, *Problems of the Feminine in Fairytales,* (New York: Spring Publication, 1972), p. 82.

[13] Paul Tillich, *The Courage to Be* (New Haven: Yale University Press, 1952), p. 81.

[14] Adrienne Rich, "The Phenomenology of Anger," *Selected Poems* (New York: W. W. Norton, 1978), p. 31.

[15] Margaret Fuller, *Woman in the Nineteenth Century in Feminism: The Essential Historical Writings,* ed. Miriam Schneir (New York: Vintage Books, 1972), p. 68. Note that Fuller's manifesto faces a sexual oppression whereas, in Joyce's writing, the issue of gender need not *be* an issue.

[16] Eudora Welty, *The Eye of the Story,* (New York: Random House, 1970), p. 305.

[17] Welty, p. 308.

[18] Anne Sexton, *Transformation,* "The Maiden Without Hands," (Boston: Houghton Mifflin, 1970), p. 83.

[19] F. Scott Fitzgerald, *The Great Gatsby,* (New York: Charles Scribner's Sons, 1925), p. 120.

[20]Olga Broumas, "Cinderella," *Beginning With O.* Vol. 72, (New Haven: Yale Series of Younger Poets, 1977), p. 58.

[21]C. L. Haupt, "On *Transformations*," *Anne Sexton: The Artist and Her Critics,* ed. J. D. McClatchy, (Bloomington: Indiana University Press, 1978), p. 147.

[22]Anne Sexton, *Transformations,* (Boston: Houghton Mifflin Company, 1971), p. 57.

[23]Vernon Young, "On *Transformations*," *Anne Sexton: The Artist and Her Critics,* ed. J. D. McClatchy, (Bloomington: Indiana University Press, 1978), p. 149.

[24]Anne Sexton, "The White Snake," *Transformations,* p. 15.

[25]Broumas, "Artemis," p. 24.

[26]Kay Stone, "Things Walt Disney Never Told Us," *Women and Folklore,* ed. Claire R. Farrer, (Austin: University of Texas Press, 1975), p. 44.

[27]Mary Ellmann, *Thinking About Women,* (New York: Harcourt Brace Jovanovich, Inc., 1969), xi.

[28]Mary Ellmann, *Thinking About Women,* p. 7.

[29]Charlotte Perkins Gilman, "Woman and Economics," in *The Roots of American Feminist Thought,* ed. James E. Cooper and Sheila McIssac Cooper, (Boston: Allyn and Bacon, Inc., 1973), p. 200.

[30]Frederich Engels, "Origin of the Family, Private Property, and the State," *Feminism: the Essential Writings,* ed. Miriam Schneir, (New York: Vintage Books, 1972), p. 193.

[31]June Sochen, *Herstory,* (New York: Alfred Publishing Co., Inc., 1974), p. 220.

[32]Sochen, p. 220.

Aphrodite Unencumbered: Kate Chopin's *The Awakening*

> "She too is a law of Nature—there is
> no law stronger than she is."
>
> "Song of the Broad Axe"
> Walt Whitman

The shifts and thaws and freezes of any century account, in part, for our loss of certain works of fiction and poetry and research; the sheer weight of production in any one of these areas justifies our expecting an avalanche. That more works by women are lost than works by men might cause more than geological confusion, of course, but useful reclamation work undertaken in the past two decades has recovered some remarkable buried treasure: Mary Webb's *Precious Bane,* Zora Hurston's *Their Eyes Were Watching God,* and Elizabeth Cady Stanton's *The Woman's Bible,* for example.

One small fictional work seems a pearl beyond price, yet this novel was buried for nearly a century under the opprobrium of outraged critics: Kate O'Flaherty Chopin's *The Awakening.* Nor has this novel's reclamation been greeted with universal agreement regarding its characters and themes. Its powers to confound, provoke, and inspire remain.

Even today, *The Awakening* invites widely disparate opinions and encourages outrage, although precisely what seems outrageous shifts from consciousness to consciousness. Edna Pontellier, the handsome and rebellious protagonist, commits adultery, abandons her children, and embraces suicide. She is acclaimed, at once, the consummate Existentialist, the modern Aphrodite, the prototypic "new woman," and the embodiment of Marxist domestic theory. No two readers interpret Edna's actions in precisely the same way.

The only thing these avid debaters of *The Awakening* agree to agree upon is that this is a jewel in the Muse's diadem. This candid, balanced presentation of one woman's rebellions against convention has been reviled as "language unfit for publication"[1] and acclaimed as "a novel uncommon in its kind as in its excellence."[2]   During the many years separating the first from the second opinion, Kate Chopin's entire literary achievement seemed quite as "at sea" as her controversial Edna Pontellier. *The Awakening*, in fact, literally killed Kate O'Flaherty Chopin.

Chopin witnessed her own demise: she suffered a literary and social shunning as enraged and more sustained than that suffered by D. H. Lawrence two decades later.   Why this venomous response to such a well-crafted novel and toward such a notable writer as Kate Chopin?   Society at that time was certainly accustomed to attacks against the status quo. Revealing oppressions imposed by class, by industrialization, by color, by sex was a fashionable and passionate subject. Edith Wharton and Stephen Crane and Henry James and Theodore Dreiser were hardly composing encomiums to social convention and marriage.

In fact, Warner Berthoff notes in his study of literature between 1884 and 1919 that realism and the "problem novel" declared a "profound though often subtle rebellion, a movement of spirit directed against particular and identifiable fears . . . and visions of the future."[3]   Writers reflected upon the changes wrought by revolutionary scientific thought; their fictional characters conveyed this perilous consciousness in an age which debated the very existence of God and the very necessity of moral conduct.

Add to this fictional chorus the voice of Mrs. Edna Ponteiller who ponders nothing less than her place in the universal order:

> Mrs. Pontellier was beginning to realize her position in the universe as a human being, and to recognize her relations as an individual to the world within and about her.

Weighty stuff. Nor would readers of Kate O'Flaherty Chopin, then and now, expect less heady considerations; her entire opus reflects a vigorous and confident engagement with the most controversial and difficult issues of her day.

Her first novel, *At Fault* (1897), unflinchingly examines men, women, and alcohol as well as men, women, and divorce without resorting to reducing the characters or the difficulties. Chopin creates no outright villains, no outright victims; her characters, even in the naturalistic fervor of the 1890's, maintain direction and responsibility for their lives.

Nor are her short stories less daring; her first collection, *Bayou Folk* (1894), reveals her broad, inclusive racial interests. Her fictional Natchitoches Parish—the imaginary, geographical equivalent of Faulkner's Yoknapatawpha County, as so many critics note—includes characters and conflicts drawn from "every race and admixture of race that can be evolved from American, French, Spanish, Indian, Negro."[5] For example, "La Belle Zoriade" studies injunctions against racial and emotional freedom; the mulatto Zoriade cannot freely choose the ebony, "le beau Mezor" because her owners have primed her for "something better." This story, which Chopin refuses to treat as a maudlin one, deals with rebellion, madness, and death and is as poignant as that of the classic, Veronese lovers.

In dealing with Creoles and the strict French Catholic mores, Chopin proves fearless and informed. "Athenaise" follows a restless, newly married woman through her dissatisfactions with that state, her journey to freedom, and her return to domestic confines. The leaving of respectability and responsibility—as conventionally defined—seems to have held a lifelong fascination for Kate Chopin. In "A Respectable Woman," for example, she handles the explosive issue of female infidelity and, in "The Kiss," writes with stunning candor of sexual desire and its gratifications.

These controversial issues and characters—bolstered by lavishly detailed settings and earnest, significant dialogue—earned Chopin publication in the finest journals of her day: *Century, The Atlantic Monthly, Harper's Weekly.* Yet, as Per Seyersted traces in his marvelous critical biography of Kate Chopin, with the publication of *The Awakening* in 1899, every story and novel that she had ever composed was removed from libraries, from bookstores, from sight.

By 1904, Kate Chopin suffered a physical decline commensurate with her literary one. While attending the famous and futuristic Chicago's World Fair, Chopin's heart collapsed, and hers was not a weak one. She had, after all, raised six children alone, her husband Oscar having died when she was but 31. Never faint of heart, Chopin had handled, without asbestos gloves, the hottest issues of her day, from temperance to sexuality to divorce to miscegenation. ("Desiree's Baby" remains an important, stirring study of this problem.) Tangled and debated or quietly imposed by a society afraid of change, these were topics of unflagging interest to Kate Chopin not only because of her strong heart but also because of her moral viewpoint. She believed in the relativity of morals.

This strength proved to be her tragic flaw; Mme. Charleville, her influential grandmother, had adjured the young Kate O'Flaherty to accept life fearlessly, to look behind the mask of morality, and to understand rather than to judge. Kate Chopin's eminent biographer, Per Seyersted explains, through this old French attitude, why Chopin's education and temperament prepared her to interpret "the cry of the dying century"[6] which she heard about her in such a stunning manner.

Seyersted also notes the impact of science on Chopin's commitment to this moral relativity. The nature of responsibility, of good and evil, of creation and self-creation sustained prolonged and often necessary attacks. Chopin's refusal to impose one limiting ethical dictum, her refusal to judge her characters led to her fall.

For refusing, to be precise, to condemn Edna Pontellier's choices in *The Awakening*, Kate Chopin was exiled from literary society and from the St. Louis circles to which she and her family had belonged. This loss, in turn, permanently impoverished American letters. By 1930, in fact, the *Dictionary of American Biography* acknowledged, in its decorous manner, how costly was this literary murder of Kate Chopin:

> It is one of the tragedies of recent fiction that Mrs. Chopin should have written the novel *The Awakening* two decades in advance of its time, that she should have been so grievously hurt by attacks of provincial critics as to lay aside her pen.[7]

But these attacks were not confined to the provinces, as this statement implies; the same Eastern journals which had welcomed her well-crafted stories castigated this meticulous novel. The relentless criticism focused not on the technical merits of the work but on the author and her fictional protagonist. Edna Pontellier received no direct condemnation

from her creator. While some critics, then and now, consider
Edna's drowning sufficient punishment for her liberation,
others—then and now—consider Edna's choosing death over
conventional life the consummate insult, the consummate
self-command.

Thus, Chopin's narrative refinement, her ability to present
Adele Ratignolle, "the mother woman," beside Edna Pontellier
and to rebuke neither character, brought down the opprobrium
of the Establishment. Only by condemning Edna or by having
Edna repent her actions could Chopin affirm—and affirm exclusively—maternity, marriage, female sexuality as conventionally
defined and experienced. But Edna says, in contrast to such
staid opinion:

> By all the codes which I am acquainted with, I am a
> devilishly wicked specimen of the sex. But some way
> I can't convince myself that I am. I must think about
> it. (216)

And this she casually reveals to her lover, Alcee Arobin; she
flaunts conventional morality not only by acting thus but by
determining to "think" about the nature of personal conduct
as if wider choices than those defined exist.

While many critics denounced both writer and character,
others pronounced Edna Pontellier a completely unrealistic
character. This opinion, of course, did little to advance the
realistic novel. And, by 1899, women such as Sarah Grimke,
Margaret Fuller, and Elizabeth Cady Stanton assuredly had
existed and often had exclaimed opinions similar to those of
Edna Pontellier. Nor was Edna, as *The Awakening* clearly
indicates, called to action by any feminist, clarion coronet.

Quite on her own, Edna comes to these deviant positions
regarding her place in a sexist world; when Leonce Pontellier
consults with the avuncular Dr. Mandalet about Edna's curious
changes, the "blue-stocking syndrome" is debated:

> She's got some sort of notion in her head concerning
> the eternal rights of women. . . .
> Has she . . . has she been associating of late with a
> circle of pseudo-intellectual women—super-spiritual su-
> perior beings?

That's the trouble . . . she hasn't been associating
with anyone." (171)

In this exchange hangs the essential horror of the tale for
conventional society. Without the revolutionary or "pseudo-
intellectual" influences of other thinking women, a woman
blessed with the best material offerings of Victorian society
might simply walk away. To Edna, social and religious man-
dates that the woman serve as wife and mother and, in so doing,
find sanctification and fulfillment simply prove unsatisfactory.

Edna Pontellier's story is simple and inexorable: a woman,
a wife, a mother, decides to abandon her former roles, to live
alone, and to become an independent artist. In the lexicography
of one generation, she is a classic "drop-out," in another's, she
is "a Bohemian," and in the most recent label fable, she is "a
liberated woman." Edna is all and none of these possibly useful
types; she is a woman with a will to change.

Yet when a female, even a fictional one, chooses herself
and her art, more debate is generated than when a real male—Paul
Gauguin, for example—decides to leave his roles as husband and
father and pursue himself and his art in Tahiti. So for the
female, social attacks against walking away from roles chosen
or imposed are swift and merciless; any one woman's choosing
otherwise simply threatens the whole equation.

The forbidden fruits of self-knowledge, self-determination,
and self-satisfaction—even regarding physical desire—attract
Edna Pontellier. Chopin uses, at this moment of incipient
awakening, a metaphor of enlightenment regarding good and
evil:

A certain light was beginning to dawn dimly within
her—the light which, showing the way—forbids it. (33)

And the voice of the sea repeats and repeats these same inchoate
messages to Edna Pontellier: "The voice of the sea speaks to the
soul" (34)

And the sea remains the single most significant symbol in
The Awakening. The great oceanic cove, the Gulf of Mexico,
is awarded both physical and metaphysical dimensions in this
novel. In this oceanic symbol, Chopin may well reflect the

influence of one of her favorite writers, Walt Whitman, who declares the sea's ability to "quiver me into a new identity."*

Chopin's use of Grand Isle, surrounded by the Gulf, seems a simple and emphatic corrolary for Edna herself: her burgeoning consciousness and her isolation. But that body of water is more, I suspect, than the usual amniotic fluid announcing re-birth. This water represents a new unity as well as a birth. Edna's task requires, after all, that she affirm body and soul in a way contrary to prescribed notions of female salvation-through-service.

The Gulf of Mexico: even in stolid, scientific language, this body of water assumes mystical powers because here the polar and the tropical waters meet. The Gulf mingles the frigid waters of the pole with the torrid waters of the Equator; the Gulf is, as many encyclopedias staidly put it, the center for "the terrestial circulation of ocean waters."

Here, in metaphorical and literary terms, the Apollonian meets the Dionysian or—for a female mythology—the Athenian meets the Aphroditian.**   Edna Pontellier's mind and soul connect where these waters mingle; in this water, Edna learns how to swim, determines to swim "farther than any woman" has ever done, and finds—at novel's end—the element for her physical and spiritual translation.

The sea centers the novel's structure quite as efficiently as it does Edna's character. The Gulf's movement is, to Edna, musical and, to the reader, circular. That is, the action of the first and the final awakening occurs on Grand Isle, in the midst of the Gulf. Kate Chopin composes a Gulf refrain, capturing the rhythmic insistence of the water and of Edna's awakenings:

> The voice of the sea is seductive; never ceasing, whis-
> pering, clamoring, murmuring, inviting the soul to wander

---

* Per Seyersted notes not only the influence of Whitman but also of de Maupassant and of Scott upon the techniques of Kate Chopin.

** I suspect I'm creating a neo-logism here; I hope someone creates it, not that we feminist critics hold any more against Nietzsche than he held against us. A feminine term correlating the Apollo-Dionysius syndrome seems timely and necessary in terms of reviewing Chopin's opus.

> for a spell in abysses of solitude; to lose itself in mazes
> of inward contemplation. (34)

Or to find itself, if the two seem mutually exclusive. This sea refrain accompanies Edna's fusion of sensual and spiritual recognitions. Her response to the Gulf's waters is entire, as is her response to music.

Beside its waters, Edna experiences her first awakening. As is the case since stories of human knowledge began, in the beginning was the Word. For the first time, Edna admits, she speaks of her childhood self, speaks, at first, in the third person and, with Adele Ratignolle's warmth and help, in the first person singular. Beside this water, Edna feels a renewal. Her sense of personal history begins with her talking openly; her sense of memory connects her with that child who wandered, freely and curiously and unafraid, through the waves of grass and away from the insistent remorse of conventional religious definitions:

> . . . sometimes I feel this summer as if I were walking
> through the green meadow again; idly, aimlessly, un-
> thinking and unguided. (43)

But the Gulf of Mexico, the voice of the sea, proves her guide. Here, Edna experiences a new life and greets death; her first swim seems to symbolize new possibilities, new powers:

> A feeling of exultation overtook her, as if some power of
> significant import had been given her to control the
> working of her body and her soul. (70)

This quest for unity of body and soul, assured by Edna's mystical connection with the Gulf's waters, is a constant theme in the works of Kate O'Flaherty Chopin.* So, too, is the idea of

---

* One cannot long study Chopin's work without noting how the term "Body and soul, free" becomes an anthem, an echo, a highly emotive refrain. Consider, for example, "The Story of An Hour" and "Athenaise" and their insistence on unity and on freedom.

stretching beyond imposed limits; Chopin examines the female's longing for the unknown, the absolute.   Note the language defying limitation in Edna's desire to swim:

> She grew daring and reckless and overestimated her strength. She wanted to swim far out, where no woman had swum before. (71)

In *The Awakening*, the Gulf of Mexico becomes the actual and symbolic center for Edna's desire for unification.   The "legend of the Gulf" which the Creole, Robert Lebrun, relates for Edna makes more apparent the significance of place.   This place is, after all, oracular for the protagonist.   On August twenty-eighth, the night of her first swim, Edna feels completely the natural wonder of a full moon: "I wonder if any night on earth will ever again be like this one.   It is like a night in a dream" (74).   And, as Edna continues to "think aloud,"—as she puts it—she finds the people around her "uncanny, half-human beings. There must be spirits abroad tonight" (74).

Robert answers, quietly and appropriately, with the legend of the Gulf: the spirit who haunts these waters seeks a being worthy "of being exalted for a few hours into realms of the semi-celestials" (74).   The fanciful Robert Lebrun seems a true prophet in adding that this Gulf spirit "will never wholly release her from the spell" (75).   While Edna wearily dismisses all this with a mild "Don't banter me," Robert has assessed her mood and her monumental change correctly.

Edna's experience in the Gulf leads her deeper into its waters, farther from known and swimmable distances.   The morning after this unifying swim, Edna determines to explore another island, farther out in the Gulf waters.   On this island, the French Catholics attend to their mystical celebrations: Mass.

> Sailing across the bay to the Ceniere Caminada, Edna felt as if she were being born away from some anchorage which had held her fast, whose chains had been loosening—had snapped the night before when the mystic spirit was abroad, leaving her free to drift withersoever she chose to set her sails. (87)

On this new island, toward which Edna has "set her sails," she experiences another affirming awakening. Far from her domestic duties on Grand Isle and upon this island of spiritual celebration, Edna Pontellier celebrates herself.

Through this trip, Chopin technically intertwines pagan and Christian details to heighten the sense of both physical and spiritual renewal which Edna experiences on this island and through the insistent sounds of the Gulf waters. Arriving with Robert, Edna decides to attend the Catholic services but finds them—like the Presbyterian worship of her youth—"stifling" and so departs. Moving toward Madame Antionette's to rest, Edna muses that this day seems a holy one:

> How still it was, with only the voice of the sea whispering
> through the reeds. . .It must always have been God's
> day on that low, drowsy island, Edna thought. (91)

Rituals of fairyland and of religion meld as Edna bathes, that is, baptizes herself at Madame Antionette's and settles royally "in the very center of a high white bed." The bed is meticulously described; it is the bed from romantic tales of princesses and peas and princes:

> The whole place was immaculately clean, and the big,
> four-posted bed, snow-white, invited one to repose. (92)

Repose claims Edna Pontellier; the scene of her awakening is sensual and precise as she discovers, and blesses, her own body:

> She looked at her round arms as she held them straight
> up and rubbed them one after another, observing closely,
> as if it were something she saw for the first time, the fine
> firm quality of her flesh. (93)

This may seem, to some readers, a mild auto-eroticism and, to others, a significant moment in a human's simple awareness of living in the body: in the body which is your own.

Upon awakening, the religious implication and social implications align as Edna conducts her own ritual communion. Otis B. Wheeler's interesting analysis of what he calls "The Five Awakenings of Edna Pontellier" includes a fine explication of this self-sanctification.[8]   Only after this communion and self-awakening does Edna join the patient Robert Lebrun and inquire how long she has slept.

Edna announces, in fine fairytale language: "The whole island seems changed.   A new race of beings must have sprung up . . . and when did our people from Grand Isle disappear from the earth?" (96).   Robert replies as the prince must: "You have slept precisely one hundred years" (96).   Yet, this fairy-land exchange is an ironic modification by Kate Chopin, just as the baptism and communion scenes modify the usual, religious procedures.

Her protagonist, called "la reine" throughout the novel, awakens to no prince's kiss.   She awakens by herself and for herself.   This lends power to her mystical connection with the Gulf and with this holy island; moreover, as Per Seyersted contends, Edna's waking alone and self-sufficient marks her as Aphrodite.   No mortal, after all, should presume to be the one who awakens Aphrodite, in whose service such capable persons as Chaucer has declared himself no more than "the servant of the servants of Love."

Certainly on this archetypal level, Chopin aligns "la reine" with the goddess of the foam, Aphrodite.   At Edna's birthday celebration, indeed, she is described in archetypal terms:

> Venus rising from the foam could have presented no more entrancing a spectacle than Mrs. Pontellier, blazing with beauty and diamonds at the head of the board, while the other women were all of them youthful houris, possessed of incomparable charms. (295)

As Aphrodite stands first among equals, Edna presides over her company.   And as Edna/Aphrodite is born in the sea on that August night, she returns to the sea at last.   Seyersted declares Edna "a Venus returning to the foam" and, as such, a powerful indictment of conventional restrictions against women.[9]   Her nakedness, Seyersted further insists, confirms Edna's freedom from unnatural conventions.

It is in this surrounding sea, the Gulf of Mexico, that the woman meets her archetype, that she combines the physical and metaphysical aspects of identity.   The new idea of personal order which Edna acknowledges violates the old order, the old proscriptions, the old roles. And knowledge regarding self-creation—that is, on spiritually defining the self and on physically conducting the self—might conflict with the established modes of behavior and self-realization.

Larzer Ziff's analysis of this novel and the tenor of its times clarifies precisely *why* it provoked such controversy. Besides being the most candid treatment of adult, female sexuality to date, *The Awakening* was the first American novel to consider marriage as "an episode in her continuous growth"[10] rather than the riason d'etre for her entire existence.

While the portrait of the fulfilling marriage of Adele Ratignolle is drawn with the same equanimity as are Edna's rebellions, Chopin was nevertheless regarded as an author who refused the conventional wisdom that marriage and family would remain "the automatic equivalent of feminine self-fulfillment."[11] This issue remains problematic, of course, because the entire social structure is founded on the dual pillars of marital sanctification and the romantic ideal.

The Awakening raises the fundamental question, according to Ziff, of whether our daughters should be immersed in the romantic dream or "be educated free of illusions."[12] On her awakening, Edna professes that "perhaps it is better to wake up after all, even to suffer, rather than to remain a dupe to illusions all of one's life" (292).

The "illusions" connect marriage and maternity; the illusions connect love with sexual desire. Various reviews from 1899 use images of lost "moorings" and of broken "cables" and of raised "anchors" to condemn this novel not only because half the action takes place by the sea but also because Edna cuts this connection. An article in the 1899 *Literature IV*, for example, regards Edna's death as a proper and inevitable punishment for her having left her "right moorings."

Dr. Mandalet perceives how illusion works to preserve the social system, how the biological imperative receives fantastic trappings in which to trap the female. On his final walk with the awakened Edna, Dr. Mandalet sadly allows that: ". . . youth is given up to illusions. It seems to be a provision of Nature; a decoy to secure mothers for the race" (291).

This novel questions, of course, whether the grand illusion is established by Nature or by society. By using the gerund "awakening," Chopin indicates a shift in consciousness. Involved in this consciousness, as Cynthia Griffin Wolff indicates, is the romantic ideal.   Yet in chiding Chopin for promising "a re-enactment of the traditional romantic myth"[13] which she then never completely represents, Wolff makes a strategic mis-interpretation.

To read the novel as a portrait of a woman plagued by the romantic illusion does not take into consideration the multiple ironies which Chopin employs to call the illusion itself—*not* Edna Pontellier—to task.   This princess, this "la reine," is awakened by no charming prince into a happily ever after. With Leonce, a prince surely, no eternal satisfaction has occurred for either principal, yet they enjoy the usual, respect-able, working arrangement.

With Alcee Arobin, Edna awakens to Eros, finding it align-ed little, if at all, with love:

> . . . there was neither shame nor remorse. There was a
> dull pang of regret because it was not the kiss of love
> which had enflamed her, because it was not love which
> had held this cup of life to her lips. (219)

With Robert, the romantic male proves himself incapable of defying "les convenances" involved in the Napoleonic Code (shades of Stanley!) and the Creole idea of possession. (130)

It is not Edna but Adele Ratignolle who represents the romantic ideal realized. And these fine friends, Edna and Adele, are as different as any two women are, except that both grew up suckled on the romantic illusion.   If Edna is Aphrodite, Adele is surely the much-idolized Catholic ideal: the will-less Madonna.   Adele is "the angel in the house" and the Virgin-Mother of Creole society. "Mrs. Pontellier liked to sit and gaze at her fair companion as she might look upon a faultless Ma-donna" (27).   When Edna begins her "dabbling" in art which will lead to her awakening sense as an artist, she sketches Adele "seated there like some sensuous Madonna."

Adele, then, is the fusion of the fairytale and the sacred female: Madonna and romantic damsel. With her "spun-gold" hair and her lips red as "cherries or some other delicious crimson fruit," Adele embodies the romantic female; she is innocence and sexuality:

> There are no words to describe her save the old ones
> that have served so often to picture the bygone heroine of
> romance and the fair lady of our dreams. (19)

Adele Ratignolle is, after all, the consummate "mother woman,"
and it is with Adele, ironically enough, that Edna's awakenings
begin. For in the lovely company of this representative of the
social and spiritual ideal, Edna discovers how unlike this ideal
she is.

Sharing confidences with Adele, Edna finds her disclosures
"intoxicating" as "the sound of her voice . . . muddled her like
wine or like the first breath of freedom" (48). Edna owes to
Adele the debt of camaraderie; in the ease and discovery of
conversation, Edna finds herself. Yet she cannot share with
her friend deep-seated discontents and rebellions. Adele proves
to be entirely too defined by Catholic strictures regarding the
female's place and the female's role.

So inviolable are the social conventions to this "fair damsel
of our dreams" that Madame Ratignolle announces herself unable
to visit her friend Edna. Edna's seeing Alcee Arobin is sufficient
cause for Adele's husband to discourage further commune
between the two women. Adele warns Edna that "Monsieur
Ratignolle was telling me that his [Arobin's] attentions alone
are considered enough to ruin a woman's name" (251).

Yet Edna neither rebukes nor ridicules her friend for such
stifling conformity. Madame leaves as she came, via the back
streets; she admonishes Edna: "I shan't be able to come back and
see you; it was very imprudent today" (251). Her visit attests
as much to Adele's affection for Edna as to her absolute conventionality.

Confronted by the perfect union of the Ratignolles, Edna
feels no envy, no desire to attain such a beatified state. She
does not even deliberate establishing such a union with Robert
Lebrun whose sensibilities and interests, superficially at least,
seem more kindred with hers than do her husband's interests.
Edna, on the contrary, adjudges that this perfect marriage
inspires only "ennui" (145). She surveys the union of Mr.
and Mrs. Ratignolle as "a region of blind contentment." Life
defined by conventional roles, goals, and identities Edna deems
"colorless" (145). Edna's awakenings lead her to lament, in
fact, that her friend Adele "would never have the taste of life's

delirium" (145).   The fundamental illusion that all women (all men) want to be and should be "one"* is thus obliterated.

And Edna's last visit with her friend Adele awakens her to the final bond: Edna attends Adele's accouchement. That bond—that bondage—has everything to do with children. Yet Adele Ratignolle finds each exhausting birth purposeful and fulfilling; she serves biology blindly, selflessly. Adele never questions convention, finds only praise for her marital and biological service. Adele's final command that Edna "Think of the children" echoes like a death sentence upon Edna.

Only the love for one's children and the responsibility toward them seem unalterable and inescapable to Edna. Etienne and Raoul, soon to return from vacationing with Grandmother Pontellier, loom like tyrants over Edna's freedom. She recognizes the social entrapment; to exercise her own personal freedom is to doom her children to social ostracism:

> The children appeared before her like antagonists who
> had overcome her; who had over-powered and sought
> to drag her into the soul's slavery for the rest of her
> days. (300)

This seems a revolutionary opinion since Genesis (and the fairytale equivalent) projects the notion that women bear children as a form of expiation for having tasted the fruit of knowledge.

Little wonder that readers in 1899 declared Edna "unnatural."   In *The Awakening*, Edna's right to be Edna is as justly presented as Adele's right to be Adele. Edna plucks down the knowledge of good and evil, relishes the taste, reassesses what husband and children and respectability mean, believes in her own identity enough to die for its free expression, and receives, not unsurprisingly, the calumny of men and women alike in so doing.

> Had she lived by Prof. William James's advice to do one
> thing a day one does not want to do (in Creole society
> two would perhaps be better), flirted less and looked

---

* Alcee Arobin proves the male's freedom to refuse the ideal.

> after her children more, or even assisted at more ac-
> couchements—her chief d'oeuvere in self-denial—we need
> not have been put to the unpleasantness of reading about
> the temptations she trumped up for herself.

This 1899 review of *The Awakening* in the *Nation* captures the
social outrage.   But temptations, like restrictions, are most
usually defined and established by society, by religion.

And religion, like marriage, insists on the female's fulfillment through motherhood; Edna is not the fairytale/mythic
embodiment of maternal womanhood; Adele is.   Adele finds
wifehood and motherhood, as Bruno Bettelheim calls these
oddly fused possibilities, "the summit of femininity."   Yet
Edna Pontellier, also wed, bred, and standing on this summit
declares herself afforded a view of still more intriguing regions.

Yet the children in *The Awakening* merit—as is absolutely
the case with children—attention.   Children are keys to their
parents' characters; through James and Cam, Mrs. Ramsey
is revealed and through Paul Morel, Gertrude Coppard Morel.*
And surely the offspring of Leonce and Edna Pontellier embody
their parents' personalities.

Leonce and Edna are erratically attentive; both parents
seem now loving, now laissez-faire.   What is of particular
significance seems, of course, the question of whether a non-
"mother woman" causes emotional or personal damage in her
children. The children of such a woman (and of a "man's man"),
Etienne and Raoul, seem hearty, unspoiled, and positively
independent.   They are leaders of the other, one might almost
say, over-weaned children.

The children of Leonce and Edna Pontellier share the
bon-bons with other children, pick themselves up when they
fall, receive hugs and reprimands with equanimity.   Under
pressure of peers these brothers combine; they "Usually prevailed
against the other mother-tots" (18). So Chopin, through these
many children, distinguishes mother-women from Edna but also

---

* These quick references to Woolf's *To the Lighthouse* and Lawrence's *Sons and Lovers* do encourage a focus upon these novels, and this
novel by Chopin, regarding the parent-child nexus and its ramifications.

"mother-tots" from Edna's children. And neither women nor children seem to suffer damages through diversity.

This attitude toward laissez-faire mothering techniques might, given the Victorian credo that the "angel in the house" must be and *wants* to be at every moment responsive to the children or to the husband, have seemed threatening to Chopin's 1899 readership. Certainly, critics deplored Edna Pontellier's refusal to act the part of the "mother-woman" who "idolized their children, worshipped their husbands, and esteemed it a holy privilege to efface themselves as individuals and grow wings as ministering angels" (19).

And if Edna Pontellier is no "mother-woman," Leonce Pontellier is assuredly no "father-man." Chopin introduces Leonce amidst a domestic cacophony of parrots and children and sewing machines; he attempts to read the financial section of an old newspaper. His response to children and domestic choirs is comparable to that of W. C. Fields. Yet what besides "mother love" could excuse the Farival twins? All the guests hear, entirely too often and at unsettling volume, their rousing rendition of "Zampa" which so torments Leonce Pontellier. Yet Leonce is hardly dismissible as a comic character.

Leonce Pontellier is a complex, decent male who finds himself quite suddenly faced with opposition. He is a business-man of considerable reputation, dedicated to preserving and observing, as he puts it, "le convenances" (130). But as spokes-man for the status quo, Leonce is neither buffoon nor tyrant; he is, rather, a responsible Victorian husband and father who, having contracted a perfectly suitable arrangement with Edna, finds her changes puzzling.

Precisely because Edna and Leonce Pontellier have managed their marriage so well—with its divisions of labor and of interest— Edna's leaving must have startled the 1899 readership. Certainly Leonce is praised and praised lavishly by the wives on Grand Isle. His enterprises thrive and expand; he shares this bounty with wife and children. The other wives pronounce Leonce Pontellier "the best husband in the world" to which, with characteristic restraint, Edna Pontellier "was forced to admit that she knew of none better" (17).

Both principals in this marriage—as in the union of the Ratignolles—know their roles and their responsibilities. Edna and Adele contract fine marriages; these characters and their unions serve as foils for Chopin, through which male and female variety is observed. The husbands are successful, mannerly men who expect emotional support and unquestioning obedience from their wives. These couples represent, to the Marxist critics, the practical arrangement outlined by Engels as that of the propertied classes. In such unions, the wife-mother becomes a decorative or aesthetic object with only limited uses and plays proletariate to the male's bourgeosie. Or, as Veblen might put it, the female becomes the model and showcase of the male's social/fiscal power. The banquet scene, Edna's birthday party, testifies not only to Edna's leaving such great luxury but also to Leonce's success in the material world.

And Leonce, because of this standard contract and its attendant expectations, cannot comprehend that Edna understands the meaning of her changes:

> Why my dear, I should think you'd understand by this time that people don't do such things; we've got to observe *les convenances* if we ever expect to get on and keep up with the procession. (130)

These are the signs of her instability: she avoids those mandatory "at homes," rides the trolleys at will, arrives home after dark without explanation, and paints dedicatedly in her atelier. Leonce fears that Edna is losing her reason, for what right-minded woman would imperil her position and inconvenience such a husband?

And Leonce is not a fool or a braggard to assume this attitude; many writings from this era indicate that women seeking self-determination were considered mad. (One thinks of Gilman's *The Yellow Wallpaper* as a sterling fictional study of this social/personal attitude and the consequences faced by the woman and her family.) Leonce explains to Dr. Mandalet his fear that Edna is becoming obsessed by the "notion in her head concerning the eternal rights of women" (170). Rather than conversing with Edna, however, Leonce continues to attend his Club, to rebuke Edna, and to reaffirm the conventions.

Leonce represents convention as, for example, does Sir William Bradshaw in Woolf's *Mrs. Dalloway*. Leonce believes in maintaining appearances; he covers Edna's move from

sumptuous Esplanade Street by announcing in the newspaper
renovation of those quarters. What is bad regarding his marriage
is also bad for business. And Leonce Pontellier is above all a
pragmatic businessman. That his wife should leave him violates
his expectations not only as a Victorian patriarch but also as
a Roman Catholic Creole, of course. That he had done
"nothing" to warrant her leaving makes Edna's actions that
much more incomprehensible.

Like Ibsen's Torvald, Leonce Pontellier can conceive of
no rational basis for his wife's discontents. Yet, despite their
having enjoyed a romantic courtship, little common interest
binds this female, this male. Yet, he once appeared to Edna as
a prince might. His Creole manners and obvious charm make
him attractive; her Kentucky manners and obvious charm make
her attractive. And that neither *should* marry the other because
of these religious and cultural differences is the most charming
detail of all, so marry they do.

Before that marriage, Edna deludes herself, or, as is
commonly averred, love is blind. She "fancied a sympathy of
thought and taste between them in which fancy she was mis-
taken" (46). Leonce finds "more diversion at the club" and,
even during his Grand Isle weekend visits, prefers the company
of men to walks with his wife, to romps with his children. Even
music, which so nourishes Edna, strikes no responsive chord;
Leonce assiduously avoids the famed "soirée musicales" of
the Ratignolles.

These two seem strangers; Edna is often alone. Yet, no
mere conflict of interest supports the burden of their marital
disintegration. Theirs is a conflict of wills. Leonce Pontellier,
in exchange for his financial providence and general good will,
demands necessary services from his wife. But although Adele
Ratignolle has no will apart from her husband's will and is,
therefore, the consummate Madonna, Edna is no Madonna.
Her awakening involves her will, her determination to govern
herself, to control her own spaces and her body. And while
Leonce is, again, no tryant, he does insist upon his prerogatives;
as she insists on prerogatives of her own, Edna and Leonce
must come to terms with the awakened will.

And Leonce receives deserved consideration by critics,
some of whom find him an eminently reasonable husband
afflicted with an increasingly libidinous wife. Cynthia Griffin

Wolff, for example, insists that Chopin has made a strategic error in constructing Leonce. He is, in fine, "a slender vehicle to carry the weight of society's repression of women"[14] and, given such a disagreeable wife, quite nonviolent.

His pattern of remonstrance and of imposing himself upon Edna is established early in the novel. Returning from Klein's one evening, having gambled and drunk copiously, Leonce wakens Edna and the children with sharp and unfounded chastisement of Edna's capacities as a mother. He comes in like a lion:

> If it was not a mother's place to look after children, whose on earth was it? He himself had his hands full with his brokerage business. He could not be in two places at once; making a living for his family on the street, and staying at home to see that no harm befell them. He talked in a monotonous, insistent way. (13)

Yet, he himself "turned and shifted the youngsters about in bed" and hears the confused mutterings about a dream ("a basket full of crabs") as the raving of a feverish child. To any experienced father, confusing the agitation of a child's dream with a child's discomfort due to illness is not common.

Leonce's outburst ends as abruptly as it begins; he sleeps soundly while the now distressed and "thoroughly awake" (13) Edna "feels an indescribable oppression" (14) from this tirade. She admits to herself that such scenes are "not uncommon in her married life;" she is, while "thoroughly awake," not yet awakened to why this encounter so distresses her:

> She did not sit there inwardly upbraiding her husband, lamenting at Fate, which had directed her footsteps to the path which they had taken. She was just having herself a good cry. (14)

And this is the language of the domestic reality: "a good cry."

This pattern of remonstrance and imposition continues; Leonce simply assumes his marital rights over her rest, over her spaces. And yet he is no remarkably tyrannical man. Consider a much disputed scene after Edna's first swim. Settling herself in the moonlit hammock, Edna reflects on the mysterious

sensations accompanying her first swim.   Her husband ap-
roaches her on the hammock, adjudges her action "folly"
because the hour is late, mosquitos abound, and his desire for
her physical attentions have been clearly established.   Edna
suddenly "perceived that her will had blazed up, stubborn
and resistant" (79).
      Edna reviews quickly many similar encounters with and
directives from her husband, Leonce:

> She wondered if her husband had ever spoken to her
> like that before, and if she had submitted to his com-
> mand. Of course she had; she remembered that she had.
> But she could not realize why or how she should have
> yielded, feeling as she then did. (80)

Edna is adamant; Leonce intractable.   Rather than proceeding
in, as she requests, Leonce joins her, sipping glass after glass
of proffered wine, smoking cigar after cigar until the realities
of Edna's positions and of Leonce's presence again press upon
her, leaving her "helpless and yielding to the condition which
crowded her in" (81).
      This scene clarifies Edna's nascent awareness of Leonce's
prerogatives and of her own capitulation to his exercising these.
As her husband, Leonce can dispel her privacy, command her
attentions, direct her physically if not spiritually.   And it is
precisely because Leonce seems so conventional a husband
that this refusal on Edna's part seems so radically to attack
the status quo.   Yet critics with a Freudian lens dismiss Edna's
rebellions as proof that her libidinal appetite has been fixed
at the oral level[15] and compliment Leonce for not asserting
his sexual rights by coercive means.
      Other readers—readers perhaps more interested in Freud
as a sexual politician—insist that Leonce oversteps the bounds
of simple human consideration.   Where he simply to exercise
the same insight and intelligence which attend him in business
and in friendship, Leonce would respect Edna's occasional
desires for privacy, for solitude.
      Moreover, through Leonce Pontellier, Chopin develops
the notions of appearance/reality which clarify characters and
their conflicts.   In this, Chopin predates women writers like
Sylvia Plath (*The Bell Jar*) and Doris Lessing (*The Summer*

Before the Dark) who employ metaphors of garment as personality. Certainly Lessing's Kate Brown creates a complex ritual of reversing clothing and, in so doing, the responses of others. This same idea of altering identity through clothing works in revealing Edna's changes:

> . . . she was becoming herself and daily casting aside that fictitious self which we assume like a garment with which to appear before the world. (148)

And this metaphor, of course, heightens Edna's last act, her final rejection of the rift between appearance/reality. Then, she sheds her garments entirely.

> How strange and awful it seemed to stand naked under the sky! how delicious! She felt like some new-born creature, opening its eyes in a familiar world that it had never known. (299)

Not until the explicit nudity and detailed sexual descriptions in D. H. Lawrence's works is so electrifying a picture of free human nature again composed. For what Kate Chopin creates in Edna Pontellier is neither a romantic tragedian nor a romantic comedian, ala Ellen Glasgow. Edna is a classic outsider.

Variously described by fictional and speculative accounts (Dostoevski's *The Idiot* and Colin Wilson's *The Outsider* and Hesse's *Steppenwolf* and Doris Lessing's *Martha Quest* come immediately to mind), the outsider perceives society in a highly unconventional way. Outsiders perceive conventional definitions of being, of good and evil, in a way which makes then unfit for conventional life. Thus, the outsider is at once the consummate victim and the consummate hero.

The outsider is enlightened: T. S. Eliot's Hanged Man of the Tarot deck or Shakespeare's Fool. At the moment of undertaking the impossible, an essential greatness redeems the insanity of the act. Cuchulain fights with the sea; Edna determines to swim farther into the Gulf of Mexico than any woman has ever swum. This heroism comes from the outsider's perception of a subtle distinction within; for example, Edna "at a very early period . . . had apprehended instinctively the dual life—that outward existence which conforms, the inward life which questions" (35).

Thus Edna, who is to all appearances the typical, well-off wife and mother, is in fact an outsider as surely as Sylvia Plath's Esther Greenwood in *The Bell Jar* or Hermann Hesse's Emil Sinclair of *Demian*.

How Chopin constructs Edna Pontellier as an outsider is rather deftly, simply achieved. First, she is not of Creole stock; their sensuality and their sexual ease startle her. Nor is she familiar with the Roman Catholic reverence for the mother-woman, the Madonna-woman; she must discern that candid talk about pregnancies co-exists with stern mores against sexual freedom.

Edna, too, has been free from the somber lessons of Calvin which surrounded her Kentucky girlhood. This Kentucky childhood has also allowed the freedoms of the "horsey-set." She knows many things the sheltered Creole women could not even suspect: of gambling, of judging horseflesh, of religious rebellion.

Edna has some financial freedom not available to the Creole women held by the Napoleonic Code; she inherits enough money from her mother to afford the "pigeon house." She can afford her freedom, too, because of her increasing reputation as an artist of worth.

Madame Ratignolle quite correctly warns Robert, early on, that Edna Pontellier is different, an outsider: "She is not one of us; she is not like us" (50). And yet Edna, for all her outsider qualities, is hardly dismissable as an aberrant creature of Kate Chopin's imagination, as the *Public Opinion* review of *The Awakening* in 1899 so ardently insists:

> We doubt, moreover, the possibility of a woman of "solid Old Presbyterian stock" ever being at all like the heroine. We are well satisfied when she drowns herself.

Ever? At all? This putatively conventional woman shows signs of being a rebel: this is her unforgivable sin. Edna is, at once, common and extraordinary. And the readers in 1899 seem genuinely torn between rebuking Edna's bad example and insisting that no such woman ever has, ever could, exist. Even the usually modulated, academic voice of the journal *Literature*

(IV) found the novel and its character "vulgar":

> The awakening itself is tragic, as might have been antic-
> ipated, and the waters of the gulf close appropriately
> over one who has drifted from all right moorings, and
> has not the grace to repent.

And the character in this novel who most encourages
Edna's rebellion might be the third principle in this female
triad of Madonna/Adele, Aphrodite/Edna. That is the crone
and artist and spinster, Mlle. Reisz, who apprehends the demands
placed upon the artist. These demands, as so often presented
in Chopin's works, make untenable the demands of the romantic
illusion.

Chopin develops this theme throughout her opus; Mlle.
Reisz finds her antecedent in the younger, more beautiful Paula
Van Stoltz of "Wiser Than a God" who chooses art over
marriage. In Mlle. Reisz, Kate Chopin completes the triad:
Madonna/Adele, Aphrodite/Edna, Virgin/Reisz. This Virgin
comes not in her aspect as Selene or Artemis, of course, but in
her aspect as the Crone, the Hag, Hecate. It is Mlle. Reisz who
embodies that artist in *The Awakening*, and it is she who shares
forbidden knowledge.

Edna's two female allies seem diametrical opposites. Mlle.
is the spinster pianist and Madame the dedicated wife/mother.
Yet, both women find passionate fulfillment in their chosen
ways. And both create through great suffering. When birthing
the etudes and preludes which so inspire the company at Grand
Isle, Mlle. Reisz's ugliness contrasts with the beauty of her
creation: "the lines of her body settled into ungraceful curves
and angles that gave it an appearance of deformity" (166).
Madame Ratignolle creates in similar contortions, her usually
lovely features "drawn and pinched," her eyes "haggard and
unnatural" (286).

Yet, these two contented women, different as they are
from one another and from Edna Pontellier, provide Edna
with knowledge. Music indissolubly links Edna with the per-
snickety and anti-social Mlle. Reisz. And for Mlle. Reisz, Edna
is "the only one worth playing for" on the whole of Grand Isle.
Like the sea itself, music evokes the "strange, new voices"
within Edna. In her most turbulent moments of change, Edna

seeks out Mlle. Reisz: "that woman, by her divine art, seemed to reach Edna's spirit and set it free" (204).

But Mlle. Reisz does not allow Edna to entertain any illusions about life as an artist. When first re-dedicating herself to painting, Edna rather blithely pronounces herself an artist, to which Mlle. Reisz responds: "You have pretensions, Madame." Pressed for an opinion regarding Edna's ability to become a serious artist, Mlle. Reisz shares some forbidden knowledge. The artist, after all, must defy convention and expect few normal rewards. An artist must, Reisz insists, "rise above the level plain of tradition and prejudice" (217).

And she evaluates Edna directly:

> I do not know you well enough to say. I do not know
> your talent or your temperament. To be an artist includes
> much; one must possess many gifts—absolute gifts—which
> have not been acquired by one's own effort. And, more-
> over, to succeed, the artist must possess the courageous
> soul." (165)

To Reisz, the courageous soul is one which "dares and defies."

Mlle. Reisz shares the knowledge of the good and evil experienced by the artist: the creation of art versus the absolute dedication of the artist. And Reisz is considered, by various others in *The Awakening*, demented, odd, insufferable. Yet Mlle. Reisz, like a good Crone, does correctly prophesy the overwhelming commitment which art places upon the artist. Edna's increasing dedication leads her away from wifely duties. Accepted as Laidpore's student, her art reflects her changes as it "grows in force and individuality" (207).

And it is through Mlle. Reisz that the profound bird symbolism unites the mother-women and the caged birds and the artist-women. This strange woman checks Edna not for the wings of those "ministering angels," the mother-women, but for wings of the artist-woman. For the artist, to Mlle. Reisz, is "the bird that would soar" (217).* Her metaphor

---

* To underscore, again, the wide divergence of critical opinions about this book, I must mention a fine article by Ruth Sullivan and Steward Smith

for the artist seems a fateful one when Edna enters the sea, glimpsing overhead the "bird with a broken wing" who, like Edna, can no longer soar above tradition and prejudice.

And it is through Mlle. Reisz that Edna receives fair warning about her romantic illusions regarding Robert Lebrun. If it is through Madame Ratignolle that Edna comes into knowledge about maternity, it is through Mlle. Reisz that she learns of Robert's true character. He may threaten, according to Mlle. Reisz, Edna's development as an artist. Reisz quite pointedly insinuates that Lebrun lacks the "grand esprit" necessary to establish lofty aspirations and to secure them despite conventional restrictions. And though Edna considers Mlle. Reisz "wonderfully sane" and capable of delivering "in a bantering way" advice which demands consideration (217), she elects to dismiss the artist's appraisal of Robert Lebrun's fibre.

Yet, Robert proves himself incapable of daring and of defying. He wants Leonce Pontellier to "set" Edna "free." Edna has already outgrown that idea:

> I am no longer one of Mr. Pontellier's possessions to dispose of or not. I give myself where I choose. If he were to say, "Here, Robert, take her and be happy; she is yours," I should laugh at you both. (282)

This sounds like a declaration by Victoria Woodhull!

Per Seyersted's inference regarding Robert seems quite useful and apt; he asserts simply that Robert "pales as he guesses that she is flouting not only the French notion of a secret affair" but also the ideas of marriage and of male sovereignty.[16] In Robert, the romantic traditions of courtly love find embodiment, and this tradition, in turn, receives a necessary second look. The notions of the secret affair, the perilous pleasures of an illicit affair, the daring of the lovers are overturned; Edna wants

---

on Chopin's "narrative stance," as they call it. They interpret the Reisz/ Pontellier conversation on the "soaring bird" as a talk not about the woman artist but on Edna's illicit passion. I disagree; the article is, nevertheless, provocative. See *Studies in American Fiction*, I, No. 1 (1973).

Robert, surely, but not on the sly. Nor does she want another, a new, husband.   For Robert, such knowledge warrants no forgiveness; understanding, too, is beyond this distressed, conventional, romantic, sensitive fellow.   Mlle. Reisz correctly apprehends his inability to embrace the unconventional.

Edna's deepest offense is her heedless quest for her own identity.   As St. Clement of Alexandria warns, a woman is forbidden this: "it is shameful for her to ponder her nature, since through her nature sin entered the world." Edna's tasting the forbidden fruit of self-knowledge changes her life.   Intent on establishing her own code, Edna questions the basic social/spiritual assumptions regarding the sexes.   She dismisses the notion that marriage alone sanctifies desire; she violates certain taboos usually employed to connect love and duty.   The forbidden fruit of sexual pleasure teaches her that physical desire is both powerful and ephemeral; possessing even Robert would initiate, simultaneously, separating from him.   That marriage and motherhood are the *sine qua non* for the female seems a dream from which—at great personal cost—Edna awakens.

> "The years that are gone seem like dreams—if one might
> go on sleeping and dreaming—but to wake up and find-
> oh! well! perhaps it is better to wake up after all, even
> to suffer, rather than to remain a dupe to illusions all
> one's life." (292)

Edna hardly certifies the unconditional happiness awakening brings; in this, she is more honest than the romantic illusions/ideals from which she has recently awakened. And in creating a character like Edna, Kate Chopin continues and extends her own artistic commitment to present:

> . . . human existence in its complex, true meaning,
> stripped of the veil with which ethical and conventional
> standards have draped it.[17]

The Nation pronounced an obituary over Edna Pontellier and her author which echoed the opinions of many readers in 1899: "as she swims out to sea in the end, it is hoped that her example may lie for ever undredged." But a few, able critics refused to deep-six this remarkable work. Edmund Wilson noted the parallels between Chopin and D. H. Lawrence; their approach to nature symbolism and their candid presentation of human sensuality seem kindred. And Kenneth Eble insisted on *The Awakening*'s being considered "a first-rate novel, and we have few enough novels of its stature."[18] More recent critics, from Per Seyersted to Carol Christ to Cynthia Griffin Wolff, have contributed to the lively academic debate of Chopin's achievement, themes, position in American letters.

In his monumental study, *The Development of the American Short Story*, F. L. Pattee regards Kate Chopin "as a vivid episode, as brief and intense as a tropic storm"[19] and could not have suspected how that storm would blow over the Gulf and return with such literary force nearly one hundred years later. But Pattee also uses the term "literary impressionism" in his 1923 study, and I can find no earlier application of this term to Chopin's works.

Literary impressionism is, of course, precisely the term for Chopin's technique.[20] And Chopin blends this impressionistic skill with the meticulous detail demanded by realism and local color movements. Her novels seem rivalled for their beauty and exactitude only by the novels of F. Scott Fitzgerald. And, interestingly enough, Fitzgerald, too, was an early reassessor of the romantic illusion.

Many teachers and critics salvaged the works of Kate Chopin when this was not the fashion, when the Wheel was still in spin, as it were. Critics of the '70's and '80's imbue the sizeable Chopin critical bibliography with their own peculiar brand of Marxist or Freudian or Feminist or Existential or Structuralist suppositions. Diverse criticism breathes continuing life into great literary achievements.

That literature, world-wide, celebrates the renegade, the seeker of knowledge, the outsider is among the proudest traditions of the art. That Kate Chopin dared to present a female in quest of self-governance is among the proudest traditions of literature by women. Edna Pontellier finds her own, controversial way past the dragons of religious and social definitions which threaten women.

By using the fairytale metaphors and the religious parallels which unite this work, Chopin assesses the dimensions of possible identity. This worthy novel, *The Awakening*, is but one of her contributions to the fuller understanding of one imperative. Despite sex or color or economic status or geographic influences, the quest for knowledge of good and evil, for self-governance, is a human one. No price is too high to pay for such "forbidden fruit."

Notes

[1] "Books of the Week," *Providence Sunday Journal,* June 4, 1899, p. 15.

[2] Kenneth Eble's Introduction to Kate Chopin's *The Awakening,* (New York: Capricorn Books, 1964), p. xiv.

[3] Warner Berthoff, *The Ferment of Realism: 1884-1919,* (New York: The Free Press, 1965), p. 5.

[4] Kate Chopin, *The Awakening,* (New York: Capricorn Books, 1962), p. 33. All citations taken from this text; pagination follows quotation.

[5] "Recent Novels," *The Nation,* Vol. 59, No. 1513, 1899, p. 488.

[6] Per Seyersted, *Kate Chopin: A Critical Biography* (Baton Rouge: Louisiana State University Press, 1969), p. 84. Seyersted's work on Chopin proves insightful, well-researched, and engagingly composed.

[7] D. A. Dondore, "Kate Chopin," *Dictionary of American Biography,* 1930 ed., pp. 90-91.

[8] Otis B. Wheeler, "The Five Awakenings of Edna Pontellier," *The Southern Review* 11, (1975), pp. 188.

[9] Seyersted, p. 160.

[10] Lazar Ziff, *The American 1890's: Life and Times of a Lost Generation* (New York: The Viking Press, 1966), p. 304.

[11] Ziff, p. 304.

[12] Ziff, p. 304.

[13] Cynthia Griffin Wolff, "Thanatos and Eros: Kate Chopin's *The Awakening,*" *American Quarterly* XXV (1973), pp. 449-471.

[14] Cynthia Griffin Wolff, "Thanatos and Eros: Kate Chopin's *The Awakening,*" *American Quarterly* XXV (1973), pp. 449-471.

[15] Cynthia Griffin Wolff, p. 461.

[16] Seyersted, p. 144.

[17]Seyersted, p. 84.

[18]Kenneth Eble, Introduction, *The Awakening,* by Kate Chopin (New York: Capricorn Books, 1964), p. vii.

[19]F. L. Pattee, *The Development of the American Short Story* (New York: Harper & Bros. Publishers, 1923), p. 325.

[20]Kenneth Eble remarks Chopin's impressionistic technique in his able introduction: "The way scene, mood, action, and character are fused reminds one not so much of literature as of an impressionist painting, of a Renoir with much of the sweetness missing." xi.

Selma Lagerlöf's *The Treasure*: Ancient Ethics

By 1904, when she composed a small, classic work entitled
The Treasure, Selma Lagerlöf's international reputation was
already established. By the 1890's in fact, Lagerlöf and three
compatriots—Verner von Heidenstam, Erik Karlfeldt, and Gustaf
Froding—had ascended "the rejuvenated Swedish Parnassus."[1]
Sweden enjoyed a new, literary Golden Age under the direction
of these writers, "the Great Four," as they are proclaimed
in Swedish letters.

Led by von Heidenstam's exuberant "avowal of other gods
than those of realism and utility and social pathos,"[2] the Great
Four determined to balance innovation with tradition, realism
with romance. In thus rejecting the unrelieved pessimism of
August Strindberg who "uncovers and delineates the worm-
eaten, the morbid, the evil in humanity," these authors sought
"the higher and redeeming motives" for human action.[3]

While many *fin d'siecle* literary movements apprehended
this need for balance, Sweden's writers seem closely aligned
with another famous literary renaissance movement: the Irish
Renaissance. Specifically, both nations raptly attended vigorous
and national new voices: the "Great Four" in Sweden, Yeats
and Synge and Lady Gregory in Ireland.*

Both renaissance movements reinstated and honoured
the history and legends and mores of their cultures. Their
writers attempted to celebrate homely details and values rather
than to escape into the foreign, the exotic, and the hedonistic.
Both nations might reasonably be cited, in Tillyard's still useful

---

* As with Lady Gregory's passing in Ireland, Selma Lagerlöf's Varmland mourned "one of the last to carry on the old aristocratic tradition that
to be of gentlefolk meant to assume responsibility for others." *The
American-Scandinavian Review*, XXVIII (1970), p. 141.

term, "epic areas" because shared language and legends and beliefs defined their peoples. And, as Dorothy M. Hoare determined in her classic analysis of Morris, Yeats and the Nordic tradition, these two cultures enjoyed and preserved "a long oral tradition."[4]

In this long oral tradition and in the great Icelandic epic form—the Saga—Selma Lagerlöf was an initiate. Her immersion in these traditions came about in a most peculiar way; her command of oral and written epic traditions might well be considered the result of, in Edmund Wilson's term, a "Philoctetean wound." At the age of four, Selma Lagerlöf suffered paralysis.

Her years of recovery, under the care and tutelage of her Grandmother and her Aunt Ottiliana, were years of initiation. According to Lagerlöf's autobiographical accounts, (collected in three highly praised volumes: *Marbacka, Memories of My Childhood,* and *The Diary of Selma Lagerlöf*) these two influential women recognized in her, even at this early age, the imaginative yet disciplined quality of mind essential to such oral tradition.*

And with this training, Lagerlöf also received vast resources in the literary epics and romances. The libraries at Stromstad and Marbacka, her childhood homes, included works by Runeberg and Tegner, Scott and Anderson. Voracious reading was to mark her character life-long; thus Alrik Gustafson, for example, can trace the later influences of Thomas Carlyle upon Lagerlöf's style. Through such education in the oral and literary traditions, Selma Lagerlöf became the great modern writer of saga.

With the publication in 1891 of *Gosta Berling Saga*, Selma Lagerlöf—the only one of "the Great Four" to reinvigorate

---

* In recalling Frau Katherina Viehman (from whom the Brothers Grimm garnered so many tales), Wilhelm Grimm noted: "She retains fast in mind these old sagas which talent she says is not granted to everyone." Joseph Campbell reviews this famous collaboration in several works, including *The Flight of the Wild Gander* (Chicago: Henry Regrery Company, 1951), p. 9.

prose—rather than poetry—gained instantaneous attention. The highly regarded critic, Oscar Levertin, who had valiantly support-ed von Heidenstam's call for an affirmative and intelligent liter-ary renaissance, considered this saga the highest representative of the new aesthetic:

> It is a style of the heroic legend that is attained here—I, poor fellow, am too blase, as we all are, too much occupied with modern life. . . . But there she sits, Froken Lagerlöf . . . who has lived alone and has a whole forgotten and concealed provincial mysticism inside her.[5]

This remark is both insightful and amusing; while Levertin noted the heroic element which was to characterize all Lagerlöf's writings, he did not yet apprehend her modernity. Lagerlöf was to handle, in this ancient, saga mode, the hottest issues of that day: pacificism, industrialization, feminism, temperance, nationalism, socialism. And while Lagerlöf certainly contained within her the oral and literary tradition of Scandanavia—almost entire—she was hardly the reclusive Greta Garbo of Swedish letters. (This assumption that spinster-writers are "there she sits" women—Emily Dickinson, for example, or Jane Austen—is quite ludicrous. As a traveler, teacher, active feminist, in fact, it seems more a wonder that Selma Lagerlöf had time to write at all, much less so voluminously.)

But Levertin's appreciation of Lagerlöf should hardly be disdained; he greatly advanced her critical reputation, as did George Brandes' review of *Gosta Berling Saga*. (His name is one familiar to many intellectual historians, as well as to many literary scholars of nineteenth century society.) Of course, any list of literary masters during the latter half of the nineteenth century reads like a Scandanavian "Who's Who." Henrik Ibsen, a Norweigian, helped to forge the drama of realism; August Strindberg, a Swede, experimented with both naturalist and expressionist theater. Frederika Bremer, proclaimed "the Swedish Jane Austen," achieved for the domestic novel what her English counterpart achieved.*

---

*Bremer's reputation in the U. S. is political; she parallels the Pank-hursts of Britain, Anthony/Cady Stanton of the States. Her novels include *Grannarne* (on familial relations) and *Hemmet* (on women's employment rights). From 1849-51, Bremer toured the USA, espousing Feminism and Art.

And George Brandes, a Dane, composed his voluminous *Main Currents of Nineteenth Century Thought,* which remains a touchstone of European literary and intellectual influences. It was this George Brandes, too, who discovered and promoted two authors of lasting merit: Henrik Ibsen and Selma Lagerlöf. Brandes declared himself deeply impressed by "the startling strangeness of its [*Gosta Berling Saga*] material and the originality of its form."[6]   And yet, the basic material—the ventures and the misadventures of the Varmland district folk during their heyday—hardly seems strange. Yet, because Lagerlöf combines, always, realistic detail with the apparatus of legend and the saga's narrative voice, the material and the form seemed startling indeed.

Lagerlöf maintained the traditional focus of the saga, centering either on a specific place or on a specific clan. Thus, for example, *Gosta Berling Saga* examines life in one province and is duly considered "the epic of Varmland." Her two-volume classic, *Jerusalem* (1901-02)—which is also translated as *The Holy City*—is considered the epic of the Swedish peasant because it focuses on the Ingermarssen clan. It is *Jerusalem* which won Lagerlöf accolades as "the incomparably greatest novelist who has written in Swedish."[7]   Even after decades of scrupulous criticism, *Jerusalem* is still considered "a monumental study of the clash between an ancient conservative peasant traditionalism and modern religious sectarianism," all achieved with what Alrik Gustafson calls "that sovereign narrative skill" so characteristic of Lagerlöf's opus.[8]

The balanced portrayal of tradition and modernity earned Lagerlöf a reputation as "a modern of Moderns."*

> One feels of her, preeminently, that she has lived in this
> age, in the twentieth century, and that she knows by

---

* Lagerlöf's reclamation of cultural myths and heroic parallels adds to one's sense of her modernity. Writers of this century reflect the influences of Sir James Frazer's *The Golden Bough,* of J. E. Harrison's *Themis,* of the enormous collection and collation by the Brothers Grimm, and of Jesse Weston's radical work, *From Ritual to Romance.*

actual experience its problems and its hopes.[9]

Certainly Lagerlöf's works focus on problems facing her contemporaries; as she exclaimed: "Everything that concerned
education, peace, temperance, the woman question, and the
care of the poor riveted my attention."[10] These issues provided
the moral dilemmas of her day, and the saga, it must be
remembered, is a didactic form of literature.

In Lagerlöf's works, the lively, common, solid men and
women of daily life face the ethical dilemmas. They receive
knowledge, willingly or unwillingly. They act; they accept
responsibility for knowledge of good and evil. As always in
modern literature, the temptation *not* to decide, *not* to assume
responsibility lures her protagonists. As with some Existential
heroes of more recent times, procrastination sometimes poses
as deliberation; negation of individual effectiveness sometimes
excuses inaction.

This moral tension in Lagerlöf's writings proclaims her
modernity; yet as a composer of highly didactic sagas, Lagerlöf
confronts ethical issues unflinchingly. The simplicity of her
style—nowhere more in evidence than in *The Treasure*—should
not be considered simple-minded, however. As Tillyard
stipulates, the narrative simplicity which characterizes the saga,
is a technique demanding precision and control:

> For all the simplicity of style, and indeed because of
> the strength this simplicity betokens, the clashes of
> character and the perplexities into which the persons of
> living drama must fall are wonderfully rendered.[11]

In *The Treasure,* two parallel plots intertwine: that of
romance and that of murder. The ancient, human need for
love presses against the age-old human responsibility for justice.
Within one fourteen-year old girl, the aspects of a cinderbound
Cinderella meet those of an heroic Antigone. Nor is the erstwhile prince less complex a character: his is the face of death as
well as of love.

The moral dilemma is heightened by Lagerlöf's refusal to
reduce the decision to a Manichaean one. Two potential "goods"
strive within the protagonist: that of redemptive love and that
of social justice. This same sophistication marks Lagerlöf's

most sophisticated sagas, *Jerusalem,* for example, and *The Out-cast* (1918), a classic treatment of the pacifist's dilemma. As Alrik Gustafson notes, Lagerlöf's ethical complexities mark both her realism and her moral depths: "The human soul is not to her primarily a Manichaean battle-ground between the power of evil and the power of good."[12] These aspects exist simultaneously; the great ethical challenge is to choose the better of two goods, not the lesser of two evils.

Thus, in this simple tale of greed and heroism and love and sacrifice, characters confront awesome knowledge of good and evil and become responsible for that knowledge. Lagerlöf's characters do not hesitate, when their consciences are properly awakened and perceptive, to judge a person or action; an ethical decision is quintessential to the development of a mature individual. The quest for such ethical maturity is a human one; no one is exonerated because of sex, race, religion, or income from moral development and responsibilities.

And to reveal motives and characters and histories, *The Treasure* (1904) combines aspects of the natural and the super-natural. All the events and characters revolve around a great casque of money. The treasure has a three-generational history, and that history proves a bloody one, indeed. As a "Soldier of God," Herr Arne stole this fortune from the great convents during the Swedish conflicts between Protestants and Catholics. The monks foretold "that this money would bring him mis-fortune."[13] This misfortune comes in the shape of three Scottish "soldiers of fortune."

When the "Soldier of God" meets the "Soldiers of For-tune," their values are unsettlingly similar. Arne Arnesson refuses to forfeit the treasure, thereby forfeiting the lives of his household. In time, this same treasure buys the lives of those soldiers of fortune when it is distributed among their compatriots. Of the principals in this novel, only Elsalill and Torarin—both of whom escape the Solberga Parsonage massacre—reject the evil spell of this treasure; they pursue justice rather than wealth. And, although Sir Archie, leader of these Scottish soldiers and the erstwhile lover of Elsalill, knows better than to suspect her of betraying him for money, he cannot conduct himself in a manner worthy of that knowledge.

Cursed money, of course, is a plot device common to all

oral and literary traditions; the moral that money, prized over
human life, accrues only evil interest is a long-proclaimed one.
That the curses upon such money are empowered more by
human avarice than by super-natural intervention is also well
known. Nathaniel Hawthorne's classic *The House of the Seven
Gables* finds excellent comparison with Lagerlöf's trilogy, *Ring
of the Lowenskolds,* in which heredity—the effects of such a
curse on several generations—receives scrutiny.

A quick paralleling of these authors might prove interesting
and better link Lagerlöf into some more familiar traditions.
Certainly Hawthorne and Lagerlöf seem anomalies because
their works are called symbolic literature or allegories or historical novels, by turns. And their novels connect dream with
reality and the natural with the super-natural. Critics finally
pronounce them both realists but in oddly symbolical language.
On Hawthorne: "He is . . a 'realist' in the only worth-while
sense of the word: in the sense, that is, that he holds a true
mirror to our common, fallible humanity."[14] And on Lagerlöf:
"This, to be sure, is not realism as the term is popularly used,
but is it not realism in the sense of presenting the realities of
life?"[15] Mix dream and legend and didacticism, and such
terminology as "realism" and "romance" and "allegory" becomes difficult indeed.

For all their uses of folk and allegorical characters and
motifs, Hawthorne and Lagerlöf firmly ground their works in
local scenes, and popular customs, and regional histories. For
both writers, this penchant for local detail is usually attributed
to the influence of Sir Walter Scott. And obvious, too, is the
influence of homogeneous cultures on both Hawthorne and
Lagerlöf. One might consider the New England of Hawthorne's
sensibility an epic area.

As Van Wyck Brooks attests in *The Flowering of New
England,* Hawthorne raptly attended "all the stories from the
farmers, tales of the supernatural, tales of ghosts, legends of
the old colonial wars."[16] And he, like Lagerlöf, incorporated
these devices and characters in his writings. Hawthorne entitled
an early story "The Threefold Destiny: a Fairy Legend," and
intended a fusion between realism and romance akin to that of
Lagerlöf: ". . . by imagining a train of incidents in which the
spirit and mechanism of the fairy legend should be combined
with characters and manners of familiar life."[17]

And in both Hawthorne and Lagerlöf, didacticism is omni-
present; this, too, seems partially attributable to their initiation
in the oral traditions of their areas. Ethical judgment and the
ability to love highlight the didacticism of both Hawthorne
and Lagerlöf. But these two write, at times, with a disarming
simplicity of style. This simplicity, as Herman Melville notes,
should not be confused with simple-mindedness. In his famous
defense, "Hawthorne and His Mosses," in fact, Melville chastized
a readership which at first dismissed such Hawthorne tales
as "Young Goodman Brown" as "a simple little tale intended
as a supplement to Goody Two Shoes. Whereas, it is as deep
as Dante."[18]

In both Hawthorne and Lagerlöf, therefore, the qualities
of simplicity and profundity seem richly aligned; they discerned
these qualities in the simple and perplexing characters about
whom they wrote. Thus *The Treasure*, a simple tale to be sure,
attains this same moral force by placing two relatively powerless
characters—a man with a palsied arm and a fourteen-year old
orphaned girl who has but recently witnessed the slaughter of
her entire foster-family—in positions of ethical responsibility.
They dispel, in utterly singular ways, the cursed money.

To place the weak or infirm in heroic circumstances is a
device common to folk traditions, according to Bruno Bettelheim. In his popular and provocative analysis of fairytales,
The Uses of Enchantment, he notes that such characterization
projects an important lesson regarding ethical development
through "the image of the isolated man who nevertheless is
capable of achieving meaningful and rewarding relationships
with the world around him."[19]

Torarin is just such a character; as a physically disabled
man, he is set apart from his fellows. "This man was infirm and
of humble condition; he had a palsied arm, which made him
unfit to take his place in a boat for fishing or pulling an oar" (3).
This introduction serves Lagerlöf's didactic purposes; Torarin—
less hearty, less bolstered by the fellowship of the sea—will
nevertheless accept the responsibility for the capture of three
able-bodied and murderous soldiers of fortune, a responsibility
from which all the other townsmen will shirk.

The males in this novel divide neatly into two camps: those
who fear to serve justice and those who value money over human
life. Only Torarin, the cripple, is morally sound, and even he

must *learn* how to live conscientiously, that is, with knowledge of good and evil and its attendant obligations.

And in true saga tradition, the dead teach the living about such ethical responsibility. The actual reflects the miraculous, the irrational the rational. And so Torarin must come into knowledge through a highly unlikely, absolutely plausible encounter with the Solberga dead. In her critical introduction to Walter A. Berendsohn's study, *Selma Lagerlöf,* Vita Sackville-West notes Lagerlöf's ability to connect the fantastic with the mundane:

> . . . wild, romantic, improbable happenings are confirmed by the thousand threads and strands attaching them firmly to a basis of sensible and homely observation.[20]

Torarin's encounter with the dead is as neatly tacked down as Sackville-West's insightful commentary could suppose.

Because he is one of the two survivors of the massacre (Elsalill, of course, is the other), Torarin feels an unshakable connection with those who, because of fate or circumstance, did not escape. And because he has taken in abandoned Elsalill, her presence is a constant reminder of his preservation. Third, his meeting with the dead occurs on the evening of the assize, the inquest into the case of the Solberga massacre. He has talked all day of that last meal and of Frau Arnesson's warnings and of his eerie escape. He has experienced delight in his unusual membership among the hearty seamen; in fine, he's a bit of a celebrity.

> Torarin had talked with many men in the course of the day; again and again had he told the story of Herr Arne's death. He had been well entertained, too, at the assize and had been made to empty many a mug of ale with travelers from afar. (40)

Rather tipsy, Torarin starts home, muttering private regret at having ignored Frau Arnesson's warnings and vowing to obey any future insight, "to hold it true and be guided by it" (41).

Within moments of formulating this half-drunken vow, Torarin encounters the dead. Despite his attempts to refute the knowledge attained through the supernatural forces, he cannot escape it. And so, when his aged and sober horse ambles into Solberga Parsonage gate and the fish-hawker finds himself summoned before Herr Arne and the household, the entire incident attains a supra-real quality so much a part of fairy and heroic tradition.

Be it dream or visitation, the encounter *seems* real to Torarin; he cannot therefore dispel his feelings of responsibility for justice, his belief in the nexus between the living and the dead. In thus grounding the supernatural in the natural, Lagerlöf achieves the intensifying current, rather than the mere shock, which flows between these poles of perception. Torarin accedes; insight informs him as he pursues, in his recalcitrant way to be sure, the murderers who, as he and Elsalill and the dead know, live as free men.

Despite his cowardly but understandable hopes that this cup of responsibility will somehow pass, Torarin finally accepts responsibility for good and evil, for the dispensation of justice. ". . . I will have no more of my conscience in this matter," he declares, and convinces the captain of the ice-bound vessel that the rapacious Scottish soldiers of fortune are aboard his vessel.

Torarin, in gaining insight, loses none of his serviceable reason. Thus, he uses the value system inherent in the crime itself to procure justice. That is, he disperses the money among the other Scottish troops to buy their disloyalty. And he uses both natural evidence (the oaken chest) and supernatural evidence (the ice-bound sea) to convince the captain that the murderers are there. Despite his final, heroic acceptance of responsibility, however, he has procrastinated too long; Elsalill is dead. The connection between the living and the dead is thus not resolved by the apprehension of the Solberga Parsonage murderers.

But before discussing Elsalill's assumption of knowledge and responsibility, it is important to note Torarin's symbolic importance to the novel. Only Torarin, of all the males in this novel, combines sight and insight and thus attains heroic dimension. The other males in this novel refuse to credit the connections between the living and the dead, the natural and the supernatural, the rational and intuitional modes of knowing.

Herr Arne is the clearest example of this dangerous dis-

connection. Frau Arnesson warns him four times of the im-
pending violence: "I am in fear of the long knives they are
whetting at Branehog" (14). The other household members,
and Torarin the guest, tend to accept her agitation and not
on altogether irrational grounds:

> They were thinking of the old mistress, how she who
> for so many years had had charge of the household.
> She had always stayed at home and watched with wise
> and tender care over children and servants, goods and
> cattle, so that all had prospered. Now she was worn
> out and stricken in years, but still it was likely that she
> and none other should feel a danger that threatened the
> house. (13)

Yet, Herr Arne dismissess her warnings on yet more rational
grounds. First, Frau Arnesson is deaf (14) and, rather than his
regarding this insistence of hers the more remarkable for that
fact, he considers it preposterous. Second, Branehog is a distance
of two miles from the Solberga Parsonage. Such information
strikes this sane man as sufficient to negate his wife's perception.
Herr Arne—for all of his being a man of the cloth and, one
might suppose, a believer in the ineluctable—dismisses the supernatural as the unnatural province of addled old women and
frightened servants.

Knowing only what limited physical senses can apprehend
stakes Herr Arne to reality and soon impales him there. He
cannot, as Torarin eventually can, balance intuition and intellect.
Nor can the villainous prince, Sir Archie, accept higher knowledge than his rational mind allows. And Sir Archie, of course,
barely discerns the importance of deciding between good and
evil. In his inability to accept irrational modes of knowing,
this Soldier of Fortune again parallels the Soldier of God.

Sir Archie represents an entire code, of course, that of the
warrior class, that of the mercenaries and soldiers of fortune for
whom money and blood-lust constitute the only values. As a
pacifist and a feminist, Lagerlöf refused to romanticize or
approve war and violence. From *The Queens of Kungshalla*
(1899) to *The Ring of the Lowenskolds* (1925-28), she employed
saga to her own didactic purposes. *The Treasure* is no exception;
the warrior's heroics receive scant praise in Lagerlöf's opus, and

in this she is an innovator of saga, as Walter A. Berendshon notes:

> In amazement we see how differently the well-known sagas are mirrored in a woman's mind, and we know that our impressions are nearer to the facts; yet there is poetic truth in Selma Lagerlöf's work for there have always been women to whose hearts the battle-frought life of men spelt horror, and little by little, this horror has dawned on the hearts of men, also.[22]

But while Sir Archie's code of adventure and acquisition receives no praise in *The Treasure,* Sir Archie is offered knowledge of good and evil, as is Torarin, through counsel with the dead who activate, at least temporarily, his conscience. The dead seek to teach him about ethics and responsibility; Elsalill's foster sister haunts him into a brief, moral awakening which he again confuses with hopes of buying off. Although Sir Archie senses the "mason" of conscience repeating: "Heart of stone, heart of stone . . . now you shall yield. Now I shall hammer into you a lasting care" (76), Sir Archie refuses this change. He judges repentance and remorse "unmanly" qualities and fears losing the respect of his fellows:

> "What would my comrades say of me if they knew I yielded to these unmanly thoughts? They would no longer obey me if they found out that I was racked with remorse for a deed there was no avoiding" (76)

This crime was made "unavoidable," as Sir Archie explains to Elsalill, because these Scotsmen were penniless, having escaped from prison where they were held for betraying the king to whom they owed service. In the final, crucial conversation between the prince and erstwhile princess, Sir Archie recounts his life, a life quite removed from conscious considerations regarding knowledge of good and evil. The material is good. Adventure is good. His code is worldly and real; his code dismisses Elsalill's as unrealistic, foolish, female:

> "If you were aught but a little maid, Elsalill, you would
> see that this [the Solberga theft and murders] was bravely

done. We acquitted ourselves like men." (135)

Yet, Sir Archie finds some recompense inescapable and, therefore, proposes to Elsalill, "That I may make good to you the evil I have done to another" (105). He offers Elsalill, ironically enough, "his" fortune, his homeland, and his name, hoping "that the dead girl may be appeased and cease to haunt me" (102). Not through his reformation and penance does Sir Archie seek peace but through possession of innocent, loving Elsalill.

Sir Archie's belief that gold can recompense evil is no more profoundly apparent than during his escape from the Taverns. After using Elsalill as a shield against the pikemen, he carries her toward the escape ship and addresses his companions:

> "Here none would give her clothes but of the coarsest wool . . . and a narrow bed of hard planks to sleep on. But I shall spread her couch with the softest cushions, and her resting-place shall be made of marble. I shall wrap her in the costliest furs, and on her feet she shall wear jewelled shoes." (142)

But Elsalill has heard these promises as a expectant bride; he now repeats these to a corpse. The silks and home and homage which the prince presents to the princess in fairytale tradition are Sir Archie's material offerings for peace of mind. His crimes are heinous and multiple.

Sir Archie ignores his true debt; he cannot allow himself to discern moral responsibility for his selfish actions. He seeks to ward off guilt and to escape punishment. He cannot exchange his lusty code for a redemptive one. When the dead foster sister realizes that Sir Archie is unredeemable, that moral knowledge inspires no responsibility in him, she inflicts knowledge on poor Elsalill who cannot recognize the predator for the prince.

Prince Charming comes to claim the needy Cinderella, Elsalill; she desperately seeks escape from squalor and loneliness imposed by the loss of her foster-family at Solberga Parsonage. Her fortunes have fallen; the prince represents position and rescue. Once the comfortable foster-daughter in the Arnesson's home, Elsalill now aids the fish-hawker and his mother in exchange for shelter. The murderer's crimes against her are both material and emotional:

> ". . . should I not remember that they have taken my
> home from me, so that I am now a poor lass, compelled
> to stand here on the cold quay and clean fish? Should I
> not remember that they have slain all those near to me,
> and should I not remember most of all the men who
> plucked my foster sister from the wall and slew her who
> was so dear to me?" (34)

Should she not, indeed; yet the murderer comes dressed in princely finery, and he is dashingly foreign, and he proposes to carry her off to adventure and security as his bride.

If cowardice stayed Torarin's pursuit of justice, then a certain moral recalcitrance also confounds Elsalill for a short while. The prohibitions against her acting on knowledge are so varied that Elsalill could easily avoid ever having to confront her ethical responsibilities. As a "little maid," she is dismissed as incapable of capturing the killers physically. This is to some extent a reasonable assumption; she is also dismissed as unrealistic when she presents evidence of the murderers' presence in Marstrand. When she rushes to Torarin—who should know better—and his companions at the warehouse, holding the large silver coin aloft, she is dismissed with a cautionary ". . . what can we do in this matter?" (82) and informed that "This is not an hour for a young maid to run about the streets of town" (82). Nor, the reader is provoked to respond, for such soldiers of fortune to roam freely.

And Elsalill is also excused from accepting responsibility by Lagerlöf's skillful fusion of Elsalill's romantic hopes and dire circumstances. Her fortunes have sharply reversed of late. That is, Elsalill "falls" from favor and is redeemed from life in the ashes by a prince. Such Cinderellas desire, as Elsalill understandably desires, ". . . that someone would come and take me away from here" (77). Lagerlöf tampers very little with such standard, fairytale expectations, yet the irony is profound.

Balancing (or unbalancing) Elsalill's hope for the romantic illusion of "happily ever after" is her expectation for justice. She has vowed to apprehend those murderers. But these two desires, for love and for justice, battle within her when she gains knowledge that the prince is the predator. She desires, of course, to reconcile knowledge and duty; she is loathe to sacrifice the only person she has come to love since the massacre of her foster-family.

And so Elsalill's ratiocinations regarding how she should deal with this knowledge of Sir Archie's true identity and of her concomitant responsibility to her dead family become fairly sophisticated for a teenager. "Were it not more pleasing to God and man," she argues, "that he be allowed to atone for his evil life and become a righteous man?" She invokes the redemptive function of love; she wants to forgive and forget. She wants love to leave him a changed man. But his lack of moral feeling and his lack of remorse make her hope untenable.

"Who can profit if he be punished by death?" she wonders, since the dead—after all—are dead. In this novel, the invisible links forging the living to the dead are stronger than steel, however. The dead profit from justice if the living do not. To Herr Arne,—who wants vengeance—and to her dead sister—who wants peace—Elsalill owes a debt as ancient as any regarded by moral literature. This debt is the inescapable obligation recognized by Antigone. The courts of men legislate against this obligation; Creon forbids her responsibility for the traitorous dead. Antigone could rest in this excuse. Likewise, Elsalill knows that the assize has closed the case regarding the killers of the Arnesson household. She, too, need not pursue justice higher than that legislated by society.

But this is didactic literature; as Antigone knows, as Elsalill knows, there are higher laws than those of men. While Elsalill may never have heard the lesson of Antigone or heard Luther's command to "Sin bravely!" Lagerlöf assuredly knew both. Her protagonists are capable of sinning grandly, even piously. Fortitude and moral clarity often force her characters into violations of established norms and codes. Thus, Elsalill will "betray" a lover and commit suicide to prevent his escaping from justice.

But in her deliberations, Elsalill also cogitates a central point in the novel: the relationship between ethics and money. Specifically, the fairytale promises financial security in the form of this prince. But what are the moral strings around this financial dream? If the princess accepts the prince's money, she also endorses how he earns that money. She is morally culpable for that, as is the prince.

This money is blood money; if Elsalill aligns her future with Sir Archie's under the mantle of redemptive love, she

accepts his value system.   When Sir Archie sends her a gold
wristband, this knowledge assails Elsalill:

> "What will my life be, if I must always call to mind
> that I am living on Herr Arne's money?" she thought.
> "If I put a mouthful of food to my lips, must I not think
> of the stolen money?   And if I have a new gown, will
> it not ring in my ears that it is bought with ill-gotten
> gold?" (112)

This seems an important issue, particularly to women who
accept male money.   The female shares culpability with the
male regarding how money is brought into the household,
whether, indeed, that money is "ill-gotten gold."   Such are
the essentials of ethical self-creation; males and females alike
create, obviously, the social values.

And so Elsalill, if she identifies her life with Sir Archie's
through marriage, identifies with his value system as well. While
she cannot do this, she rages against the knowledge given her
like a small Oedipus.

> "Had not my foster sister revealed her murderer to me
> I might have sat here with a heart full of joy." (114)

Her social expectation that she will love and her spiritual training
that she can serve God through loving a male further excuse her
rising to this dangerous responsibility.   But even a would-be
princess, if she avoids the moral vacuity which material well-
being and typical female roles can promote, must under the
proper, extraordinary conditions acquit herself as an ethical
woman.

To acquit herself as a woman, Elsalill must affirm the
sororal alliance, even at the expense of her redemptive hopes
for Sir Archie.   When she learns that Herr Arne sacrificed them
all to retain possession of the accursed money, Elsalill com-
prehends the full horror of this cyclical greed.   As she turns
the pikeman's weapon upon herself, "Now I will serve my
foster sister so that her mission shall be fulfilled at last" (138),
she does so with complete understanding of her responsibility
to and for the dead.

The foster-sister has sought peace rather than vengeance;

her symbol resides in the natural world: the birch. Elsalill
recalls a crucial conversation with her sister; walking in a spring
field one year ago, the sisters happen upon a torn sapling. The
severed birch sprouts leaves; this phenomenon provokes a
prescient debate between the sisters. Elsalill considers: "Maybe
it grows so sweet and green that he who cut it down may see
the harm he has wrought and feel remorse" (100). This is
precisely her hope for Sir Archie, a hope doomed by Sir Archie's
moral indifference.

The foster-sister pronounces, while regarding the torn
tree, the connection between all that lives and dies in the world:

> All the good they yet desire is that they be left to sleep
> in peace. Well may I weep when you say this birch
> cannot die for thinking of its murderer. The hardest
> fate for one deprived of life is that he may not sleep
> but must pursue his murderer. The dead have naught
> to long for but to be left to sleep in peace. (101)

The foster sister recognizes capricious violence and the eternal
pursuit of justice; the debate over this birch clarifies for Elsalill
the onerous responsibility still connecting her with her sister
and both of them with Sir Archie.

Sir Archie, too, has a symbol in the natural world, one
hardly fitting for a redemptive and protective male: the wolf.
Bettelheim's analysis of the wolf in folktales seems applicable
here, tutored as Lagerlöf was in the oral traditions: ". . . the
wolf is not just the male seducer, he also represents all the
asocial, animalistic tendencies within ourselves."[22]   And this
wolf image also supports the blood-lust of Sir Archie and his
soldiers of fortune. The charcoal burner, at whose Branehog
fire the rapacious men whetted their long knives reports: "I
thought I had three werewolves in the house with me. . ." (19).

But in their finery, these wolves seem elegant foreigners
to Elsalill who, in the novel's course, must distinguish appearance
from reality and come into knowledge of the true identity
much as Psyche must discern Cupid. In recounting her horrific
tale, therefore, Elsalill does not notice that "their ears grew
long with listening and their eyes sparkled, and sometimes their
lips parted so that the teeth glistened" (32). In Sir Archie,
she cannot yet recognize "the eyes and teeth of a wolf" (32).

But when she receives knowledge of his true identity as the killer of kin and yet hesitates to bring him to justice, Elsalill recognizes her own guilt: "God forgive my sin!" she implores as she confesses to herself: "I have loved a wolf of the woods . . . and him I have tried to save from justice!" (135)

The cyclical nature of this issue of identity and obligation is symbolized by the great frozen sea which seals the island of Marstrand. Through Torarin, the reader learns that the ice has never held so fast in so mild a season; nature's most powerful, elemental force thus reflects the links between the living and the dead, between social crime and social justice. Winter refuses to yield to spring; the dead will not release the living. Elsalill's indecision parallels the locked seasons; the natural world supports the supernatural world.

The novel's final scenes are played out on this frozen expanse. The captain of the icebound vessel is, in old fashioned terminology, a God-fearing man. He recalls with Torarin a similar impasse many years before in which no ship found release until a robber of churches was found aboard one vessel and returned for justice to the harbour folk of Bergen (58). So, when Torarin produces evidence of the murderer's presence on board, the captain is inclined to believe him.

The seizure scene is bawdy and horrific. Scotsmen greedily divide the treasure while others seek out Sir Archie, Sir Reginald, and Sir Philip. In unnecessary numbers and with chilling zeal, armed men rush upon sleeping men. Herr Arne's vengeance is assured; greed procures it. But the ship remains icebound: "Nothing was changed around the vessel, and the wall of ice towered ever higher before her" (158).

The circle is not yet completed; the heroic dead has yet to receive her due. Again, the living and the dead find connection and play out that union on the majestic, terrifying, frozen sea. The final scene glides quietly upon the imagination after the clangorous sounds of money and battle which precede it. The only violence in the final scene is that of the sea opening. When "all the women of Marstrand" learn of Elsalill's sacrifice and valor, they approach the vessel with a bier. The women claim their dead, understand her code: ". . . and all the women in the place wept over the young maid, who had loved an evil-doer and given her life to destroy him she loved" (150).

Such demands fall upon the individual soul and must be

accepted; the knowledge imparted to Elsalill costs not less than everything. Her valor attests the unity of sight and insight, and of irrational and rational modes of knowing. Elsalill denies herself the fairytale promises of the Cinderella legend not because such goals are improper but because both principals are not equal to the task of such loving.

The ice breaks up, the season of rebirth begins, therefore, as the procession of women bears Elsalill's body into Marstrand "with all the honour that is her due" (159). As June Arnold remarks in her Preface to *The Treasure,* this honour reverses Sir Archie's prediction that "she will have only a pauper's grave and soon be forgotten."[23] The full power of the scene combines natural and symbolic components; Lagerlöf's preservation of the essential simplicity and force of saga's narrative position here receives fine example:

> ". . . the wind and waves broke in behind them and tore
> up the ice over which they had but lately passed; and
> when they came to Marstrand with Elsalill, all the gates
> of the sea stood open." (159)

Lagerlöf's *The Treasure* indicates the didactic force in- herently possible in the saga form. She found this means, during an age of religious skepticism, to keep faith with ethical belief. Her novels testify to the ancient and modern need for individual discernment and responsibility regarding good and evil. True to her ancient form, Lagerlöf scrutinizes that moment in individual life when absolute knowledge seizes one. Asked or uninvited, such knowledge provokes binding responsibilities in the ethical being. As always, Lagerlöf studies ethical deliberation within the individual; she examines moral motivations.

If, as this tale suggests, the male must overcome specific impediments to ethical knowledge—egotism and fear and a logical harness which prevents the free motion of his intuition—the female, too, must overcome specific impediments to ethical action. She must foreswear her romantic illusions when issues of actual familial love and responsibility seem to conflict. She must scrutinize the injunctions that her love can be, in all cases, morally revivifying. The human, female or male, must insist on developing an ethical faculty, based upon the lucid and loving analysis of any perplexing circumstance. The "Treasure" may well be this ethical insistence among us, the living and the dead.

Nor is this didactic literature—which combines myth and history and place—a lost tradition. Noting Eudora Welty's *The Robber Bridegroom* and Selma Lagerlöf's *The Treasure,* I was drawn by three elements which align the novels and, in turn, their authors. First, both novels follow the basic premises of the old fairytale, "The Robber Bridegroom": the erstwhile lover is a criminal; true versus false identity is central; the female's acting upon knowledge is crucial. And in *The Treasure,* as in the fairytale, a "godless crew" slays a youngster, despite her piteous cries.

Thus, both authors seem guided by folk and fairy traditions. Welty even identifies some of the myth and fairy influences abounding in *The Robber Bridegroom:* Grimm's tale, the legend of Cupid and Psyche, the frontier tales of Mike Fink, the folklore surrounding the thieves along the Natchez Trace.[24]   As Katherine Anne Porter states in her warm introduction to Welty's *A Curtain of Green and Other Stories:*

> . . . from the beginning until now, she loved folktales, fairytales, old legends, and . . . the songs and stories of people who live in old communities whose culture is recollected and bequeathed orally.[25]

Both Lagerlöf and Welty are initiates in the rich oral traditions of their cultures. Perhaps both enjoyed living in "epic areas." It might be agreed that, while there are few such "epic areas" left in the world, one of them assuredly is the back-country of Mississippi. In turn, Welty's greatest contribution may, in time, be that of her ethnocentric imagination. She is recording, as only the great writer can record, a set of beliefs or customs or circumstances which are at once specific and universal, timeless and vanishing.

But the second (and certainly less contrived) connection between the authors might reinforce this suspicion about "epic areas" in some small, reassuring way. Welty and Lagerlöf unite local history with these mythic/fairytale components.

> ". . . it was not accident that I made our local history and the legend and the fairytale into working equivalents in the story I came to write. It was my firm intention to bind them together."[26]

While Lagerlöf could have said this very thing, this is a statement by Eudora Welty. It is included in a fascinating talk presented to the eminent Mississippi Historical Society about her novel, *The Robber Bridegroom*. Welty entitles this presentation "Fairy-tale of the Natchez Trace," and traces her integration of mythic elements, fairytale elements, history, and ironic twists.

In employing fairytale and myth, Welty employs a technique which she terms "ironic modification." This technique functions in the works of Lagerlöf, as *The Treasure* proves, but the point is interesting enough to excuse some repetition of it. Both Elsalill and Rosamund must confront knowledge of good and evil; their princes are, if not blackguards, then soldiers of fortune. Lagerlöf has Elsalill discover the "true face," the real identity of her lover; with this knowledge, all hope of fulfilling the romantic dream eludes her.

In a similar manner, Welty has Rosamund repeat what Welty calls "her version of the classic mistake" by having her seek the true identity of Jamie-Cupid. Then, Welty further modifies this archetypal moment by affirming Rosamund's act; this determination to know and then to become responsible for knowledge is affirmed in Welty. Then she further modifies the fairytale aspects of the tale by implying the "happily ever after" may not consitutue the *summum bonum,* as does, of course, Lagerlöf. As Charles E. Davis puts it, the fairytale parallel tempts the reader to assume the fairytale outcome, but Welty's consistent "ironic modification," according to Davis, "will not allow such an interpretation without consider-able qualification."[27]

As nursery fairy tales exist, Welty notes, they could hardly be considered substantial moral fare for adults: "Fairy tales don't come from old wisdom, they come from old foolishness—just as potent."[28] Welty further insists that fairytales must be transmuted by the novelists, if ethical realism is to be achieved: ". . . fairy tale perfection forbids the existence of choices, and the telling always has to be the same."[29] Such is the fairytale identity, the fairytale expectation. What elevates the tale into the folk tradition—an heroic tradition to be sure—is Welty's use of "ironic modification." Like Lagerlöf, she trans-mutes the changes traditionally defined in fairyland: prince, kiss, proposal, outcome.

In Lagerlöf, the modification is stunning; the first and the last encounter of princess/prince is literally deadly. From such "ironic modifications," Lagerlöf draws the moral complexities confronting the common, romantic female. Knowledge of good and evil is—even in the fairytale cosmogony of Eden—the primordial "ironic modification" of living happily every after. And this didactic function, so essential a component of the saga tradition, might also connect Welty with Hawthorne and with Lagerlöf.

Katherine Anne Porter, introducing Welty's *A Curtain of Green and Other Stories,* notes Welty's "ancient system of ethics, an unanswerable, indispensable moral law on which she is firmly grounded." And this ethical imperative in literature seems to be supported by the oral tradition in which, as a character, Elsalill is a plausible balance between the Cinderella aspect of the female who seeks delivery through loving the prince and the Antigone principle in the female which insists on responsible, ethical behavior. In Lagerlöf's works, the exceptional man or woman is the common, responsible, harried person who uses the knowledge of good and evil discerningly, even if this puts him/her at odds with social norms or expectations.

In *The Treasure* as in all Lagerlöf's works, how one lives, how one creates a code proper to one's own ideas of ethics is as important as that one lives at all. If essence precedes existence, quintessence surely follows it, according to Selma Lagerlöf.

> Beauty to her could not exist outside a moral context,
> and she became in consequence the great moralist among
> Swedish literary figures who appeared in the 1890's.[30]

With John Gardner's recent call for moral writers and, by inference, for ethical readers who expect examination of dynamic relationships with knowledge of good and evil, Selma Lagerlöf's star may again be ascendant. The accolades accorded her literary achievements suggest the merits of her work. The 1909 London *Times* declared her "unquestionably the most eminent of Swedish writers in an age when literature is cultivated almost to excess in Sweden." And, in an enthusiastic coda, it further proclaimed Lagerlöf "among the half dozen leading living writers in the world."

But such was common opinion regarding Selma Lagerlöf;
by 1909, she had become not only the first woman to receive
the Nobel Prize in Literature but also the first Swede. Her
works earned her an honorary degree from the prestigious
Uppsala University and a seat among the eighteen "Immortals"
of the Swedish Academy. The conservative Swedish daily,
Dagblad—as noted for hyperbolic praise as the London *Times*—
acclaimed her in nearly mystical terms: "The prophetess is
forgotten for the voice that speaks through her. It is as if the
book . . . had sprung direct from the soul of the Swedish
nation."[31]*

What Scotland hears in Sir Walter Scott, what we hear
in Walt Whitman, the Swedes—and soon the Western literary
world—attended in the voice of Selma Lagerlöf. And in such
epic work, regional details and realism in no way impede universal understanding and appreciation. The scope and diversity
and complexity of the human experience receive due representation.

Or, in Tillyard's still useful delineation of epic literature,
Lagerlöf's writings attained such popularity and influence
precisely because they proved "narrative on a large scale,"
serious enough to "merit . . . the epithet universal," and were
"positive rather than critical."[32]   Neither Scott nor Whitman
nor Lagerlöf in any way compromised their ethnocentric realism
in composing epic works.   Yet, all achieved what one critic
extolled as an "anthropomorphic imagination."

In his review of Doubleday's nine-volume edition of
Lagerlöf's works in 1917, the editor of the notable *American-
Scandanivian Review*, H. G. Leach, defined this imagination as
one produced by epic areas. Elements of lore and fact, of myth
and story, of history and legend combine in such cultures and
in such writers: "bits of folklore are as real to the Swedish
peasant as his Bible."[33]   And this blend remains a salient feature
of Swedish literature; Par Lagerkvist's *The Dwarf* (1944)
indicates—as do many novels by Lagerkvist, the 1951 winner

---

* For children of whom you are particularly fond, this book, the
children's classic *The Adventures of Nils,* is a proper gift.

of the Nobel—the continuing influence of Selma Lagerlöf.
Neither the barriers of translation—which in some cases
distance the reader from the exactitude of Lagerlöf's skill[34] —nor
the moral tepidity of recent times dilutes the pleasure and
provocation a Lagerlöf work provides.

Lagerlöf might best be characterized as, in Hawthorne's
term, an "Artist of the Beautiful," who did not suffer Owen
Warland's temporary loss of faith:

> He had lost his faith in the invisible, and now prided
> himself, as such unfortunates invariably do, in the wisdom
> which rejected much that even his eye could see, and
> trusted confidently in nothing but what his hand could
> touch.

Selma Lagerlöf, on the contrary, balanced the natural
and supernatural, believed in the ineluctable. Thus, Selma
Lagerlöf's entire opus not only examines but repeatedly affirms
our human ability to measure up to knowledge of good and
evil.

Notes

[1] Alrik Gustafson, *A History of Swedish Literature* (Minneapolis:
University of Minnesota Press, 1961), p. 290.

[2] Gustafson, p. 289.

[3] Edward J. Wheeler, "Sweden's Greatest Woman Poet," *Current
Literature*, XLVI (1909), pp. 288-89.

[4] Dorothy M. Hoare, *The Works of Morris and Yeats in Relation to
Early Saga Literature* (Cambridge: University Press, 1937), p. 1.

[5] Alrik Gustafson, *Six Scandanavian Novelists* (Princeton: Princeton
University Press, 1940), p. 186.

[6] Gustafson, *A History of Swedish Literature*, p. 30.

[7] Edward J. Whalen, "The Nobel Prize-Winner," *Current Literature*,
Vol. 48 (1910), pp. 218-19.

[8]Gustafson, *A History of Swedish Literature*, p. 311.

[9]Edward J. Whalen, p. 218.

[10]Selma Lagerlöf, "How I Turned Scribbler," *Living Age,* 327 (1925), pp. 322-329.

[11]E. M. W. Tillyard, *The English Epic and Its Background* (New York: Oxford University Press, 1954), p. 125.

[12]Alrik Gustafson, *Six Scandanavian Novelists*, p. 208.

[13]Selma Lagerlöf, *The Treasure,* trans. Velma Swanston Howard (Plainfield: Daughters, Inc., 1973), p. 12. All quotations taken from this text; pagination follows citation.

[14]"Hawthorne, Nathaniel," *Cyclopedia of World Authors,* ed. Frank N. Magill (New York: Harper & Bros., 1958), p. 489.

[15]Olga Flinch, "Selma Lagerlöf," *The Outlook*, LXX (1902), pp. 977-980.

[16]Van Wyck Brooks, *The Flowering of New England : 1815-1865* (New York: E. P. Dutton and Company, Inc., 1940), p. 216.

[17]Terence Martin, *Nathaniel Hawthorne* (New York: Twayne Publishers, Inc., 1965), p. 52.

[18]Herman Melville, "Hawthorne and His Mosses," *The Shock of Recognition,* ed. Edmund Wilson (New York: Farrar, Straus and Co., 1943), p. 202.

[19]Bruno Bettelheim, *The Uses of Enchantment* (New York: Vintage Books, 1977), p. 172.

[20]Vita Sackville-West, "Preface," in *Selma Lagerlöf*, by Walter Berendsohn (Port Washington: Kennikat Press, Inc., 1931), p. v-x.

[21]Walter A. Berendsohn, *Selma Lagerlöf: Her Life and Work,* trans. George F. Timpson (Port Washington: Kennikat Press, Inc., 1931), p. 48.

[22]Bettelheim, *The Uses of Enchantment*, p. 172.

[23]June Arnold, "Introduction to the Novel," *The Treasure* (Plainfield: Daughters, Inc., 1973), p. iii.

[24]Eudora Welty, "Fairy Tale of the Natchez Trace," *The Eye of the Story* (New York: Random House, 1970), pp. 300-314.

[25]Katherine Anne Porter, Introduction, *A Curtain of Green and Other Stories* by Eudora Welty (New York: Harcourt, Brace and Company, 1936), p. xiv.

[26]Eudora Welty, "Fairy Tale of the Natchez Trace," p. 305.

[27]Charles E. Davis, "Eudora Welty's *The Robber Bridegroom* and Old Southwest Humor," ed. John F. Desmond, *A Still Moment : Essays on the Art of Eudora Welty* (Metuchen, NJ: The Scarecrow Press, Inc., 1978), pp. 71-81.

[28]Eudora Welty, "Some Notes on Time in Fiction," *The Eye of the*

Story, p. 164.

[29]Welty, "Some Notes on Time in Fiction," p. 164.

[30]Gustafson, *A History of Swedish Literature*, p. 307.

[31]Velma Swanston Howard, "Selma Lagerlöf: The First Woman to Win the Nobel Prize for Literature," *Putnam's Magazine*, VII (1909-1910), pp. 708-713.

[32]E. M. W. Tillyard, *The English Epic Tradition*, The British Academy's Wharton Lectures on English Poetry XXII (London: Humphrey Milford Amen House, E. C., 1936), p. 4.

[33]H. G. Leach, "Miss Lagerlöf's Popularity," *The American-Scandinavian Review*, V (1917), p. 113.

[34]Lola Ridge, review of *The Holy City* by Selma Lagerlöf, *The American-Scandinavian Review*, VI (1918), p. 222. Reviewers, such as Lola Ridge, capable of enjoying these works in Swedish, commonly declare that: "Everywhere the meaning has been conveyed not only by the good but by the magic word, so that there is a complete collaboration between sound and sense."

Quest for Unity: Atwood's *Surfacing*

The present state of Canadian letters might best be described as a state of elation. Ronald Sutherland declares this renascence "Canada's Elizabethan Age," and Margaret Atwood declares it "a literary expansion of Malthusian proportions."[1] While these two are major figures in the renaissance, the remarks need not be dismissed as self-serving ones. The recent scholarly edition of the three-volume *Literary History of Canada* affirms their exuberant opinion, and even the elder statesman of Canadian criticism, Northrop Frye, who considers literature "essential to the spiritual health of the individual and the nation,"[2] declares contemporary Canada healthy.

Foremost among those creating this excitement is Margaret Atwood; in a lively interview with the writer, Ellen Coughlin notes Atwood's celebrity status:

> . . . she is hot property there. The cover of the December 31 issue of *Maclean's*—the Canadian counterpart of *Time* or *Newsweek*—displays a photograph of Ms. Atwood (unidentified) with those of about a dozen other instantly recognizable celebrities of the year just past, including Pierre and Margaret Trudeau, Jimmy Carter, Ayatollah Ruhollah Khomeni, and Jane Fonda.[3]

The public adulation of Margaret Atwood is remarkable; academic opinion, while hardly as zealous, seems generally to agree with her adoring public. Critics find in her prose, as in her many volumes of poetry, technical ability and an original style.

As an editor of the eminent journal, *Canadian Literature,* George Woodcock has reviewed the finest among Canada's younger generation of writers. In his opinion:

> No other writer in Canada of Margaret Atwood's gen-

eration has so wide a command of the resources of literature, so telling a restraint in their use.[4]

And in the concluding chapter of the three-volume, collectively
edited *Literary History of Canada*, Northrop Frye declares
Atwood's *Surfacing* an "extraordinary novel" which perfectly
represents her own critical review of Canadian themes.[5]

Northrop Frye's praise is valuable precisely because he
includes in his estimation Atwood's controversial critical work,
Survival: A Thematic Guide to Canadian Literature (1971).
The work is controversial not because it lacks either perception
or utility but because *Survival* addresses itself to the common
reader rather than to the scholarly one.* Despite its dismissal
by some members of the intellectual Establishment, Frye and
others in this same circle agree that *Survival* is "a most perceptive
essay on an aspect of the Canadian sensibility."[6]

Perhaps few readers of Frye's own critical opus register
surprise at his support; Atwood's creative and critical writings
indicate—to positive advantage—his influence upon the younger
generation of Canadians. And while I cannot present a complete
analysis of the parallels between Frye's theories and Atwood's
methods, I shall endeavor to suggest several key examples of
his influence.

What Margaret Atwood means by "survival" is manifested
clearly, according to Frye, in *Surfacing*:

> . . . where the heroine is isolated from her small group
> and finds something very archaic, both inside and out-
> side her, taking over her identity.[7]

While the issue in *Surfacing* is the reintegrating rather than the
"taking over" of identity, Frye's definition may prove serviceable. This novel is, as almost every critic and reviewer who has
ever written on the subject attests, a novel about identity on a

---

* In a 7 March 80 interview with *Books and Arts*, Atwood explains
the controversy thus: "The book upset a lot of academics—first of all
because it had no footnotes . . . and second because they felt I was poaching
on their territory."

national level and on the female, personal level.

"Perhaps," Frye ruminates, "identity only is identity when it becomes, not militant, but a way of defining oneself against something else."[8]   The protagonist examines several aspects of identity.   She juxtaposes her own historical generation with that of her parents. She contrasts how the members of the microcosm define themselves with how she does.   She confronts true memory regarding her childhood beliefs and adult behavior.   She determines to unify her body/mind dichotomy, and this is her single most important achievement in establishing an identity.

Noting the correlation between isolation and identity is strategic to an understanding of *Surfacing*.   Isolation on a physical level is assured by the journey into the wilderness; isolation from her peers is a complicated matter, however, because this generation is, itself, disconnected from both personal and historical identity.

Therefore, Atwood emphasizes the Surfacer's isolation as being primarily a reflection of her generation's disconnection. Their microcosm of two men and two women moves into a physical isolation which increasingly defines them. They travel a few hours by car, yet they enter "foreign territory."[9]   The language and customs which separate Quebec from Ontario, these English from those French Canadians, isolate these travelers. The novel's focus on isolation and identity sharpens with their journey.

That is, these four proceed deeper into geographical and symbolic separation; they move toward their final destination: an island.   They must traverse a lake "blue and cool as redemption" (18), and this water, in turn, becomes both a symbol of their isolation and of the Surfacer's purification. The water is the medium for the Surfacer's unification and survival.

This abandoned island seems a sustaining Eden for the four characters; they survive on produce from its neglected garden, on fish from its pillaged waters. The island invites peaceful contemplation and self-renewal. But only the Surfacer reexamines her connections, her personal values. Atwood's use of this highly symbolic island suggests another connection between Frye and this younger writer.

Frye's *Anatomy of Criticism* (1957) notes that certain

physical settings usually symbolize what he calls "the point of ephiphany" where "the undisplaced apocalyptic world and the cyclical world of nature come into alignment."[10]   Such is the island of the Surfacer's childhood identity against which she must now redefine herself.

This island is an oracular place for the Surfacer; here she confronts memory and her lost parents and self-knowledge. And this return, not necessarily to a previous locale but to the natural world, is a central motif in the Canadian novel noted in Edmund Wilson's *O Canada* (1964) and Northrop Frye's *The Bushe Garden* (1971).   Frye cites this "nostalgia for a world of peace and protection" as a "particularly strong" theme in Canadian identity.[11]   Atwood suggests the complexity of Frye's "peaceable kingdom" by making the Surfacer fear nature's power to reveal the human identity.   Thus, the Surfacer must bridge the chasm between the natural and urban worlds in order to achieve passage into identity.

Critic Margot Northey suggests that the Surfacer is faced with not pastoral peace but "the double menace of nature and civilization."   The isolation and quiet of the island force the character into self-scrutiny; she remembers her childhood identity as being defined "between two anonymities: the city and the bush" (62).   Northey deduces that the character's childhood emotions and adult ratiocinations conflict:

> The external conflict may in turn be connected to the internal conflict between primitive emotions and rationality displayed by the narrator.[12]

She fears this insular place where past and present collide; the Surfacer fears learning of her father's death, learning about herself, learning about her peers:

> I want to go back where there is electricity and distraction. I'm used to it now, filling the time without it is an effort. (59)

In the unnatural natural quiet, the Surfacer hears herself think; the thoughts are insistent and profoundly disturbing.   Her identity faces a test not only of survival but of renewal.

Despite her protestation, however, the Surfacer cannot

escape knowledge. After a futile weekend's search for her missing father, the Surfacer hopes the crisis is behind her.

> No one can expect anything else from me. I checked everything, I tried; now I'm absolved from knowing. . .
> (59)

But, the protagonist must reconcile herself with the preceeding generation. So driving is her need to unify with them and to understand their influences that the protagonist eventually summons the ghosts of both parents. Knowledge shared between the quick and the dead, so prominent in Lagerlöf's *The Treasure*, also provokes the character in *Surfacing*.

Yet Atwood cannot depend, as can Lagerlöf, on the saga's traditional fusion of natural and supernatural elements to make such connection credible. For this first-person narrative, Atwood must select another tradition; she specifies which quite succinctly in an informative discussion of *Surfacing* and literary ghosts:

> You can have the James kind, in which the ghost that one sees is in fact a fragment of one's own self which has split off and that to me is the interesting kind and that is, obviously, the tradition I'm working in.[13]

By novel's end, therefore, the Surfacer reconciles within herself the human balances which her parents represent. She accepts emotional balance with each parent, finding within herself her father's rationality and her mother's understanding. Gaining much insight releases her, as Atwood elucidates in further remarks on the Jamesian ghosts. She likens the protagonist of *Surfacing* to the protagonist in James's "The Jolly Corner":[14]

> She is obsessed with finding the ghosts, but once she finds them she is released from that obsession.

The Surfacer's preoccupation with family history and emotional history estranges her from her peers, who abrogate all connection with history. Her reason for returning to this isolated retreat confounds and disturbs them:

> . . . my reason for being here embarrasses them, they
> don't understand it.   They all disowned their parents
> long ago, the way you are supposed to: Joe never men-
> tions his mother and father, Anna says hers were nothing
> people and David calls his The Pigs. (19)

This generation, apparently, prefers not only to judge but also
to abandon parents.   This denial seems aberrant; these adults
seem unnatural, sprung without familial ties from their own
imaginations.   These four adults might also represent the first
barrage of the fabled "Baby Boom" yet seem disconnected
even from this historical phenomenon.

Each seems unwilling or unable to share personal history.
"My friends' pasts," the Surfacer admits, "are vague to me
and to each other also, any one of us could have amnesia for
years and the others wouldn't notice" (35).   The Surfacer thus
dispassionately assesses her contemporaries:

> A little beer, a little pot, some political chitchat, the
> golden mean; we're the new bourgeoisie, this might
> as well be a Rec Room. (46)

Each individual is isolated, preferring cliche to the risks of
personal expression.   Among these peers, too, form lacks
content, and appearance symbolizes nothing deeper than its
superficial reality.   The protagonist notes David's long hair
and Joe's beard as "just the style now, like Crew Cuts" (34).
Divorced from both personal and cultural history, these adults
seem disconnected from one another and themselves.

The Surfacer apprehends her separation from this company.
These friends are of the instant coffee variety so common to
our mobile times.   The protagonist says of Anna: "She's my
best friend, my best woman friend.   I've know her two months"
(12).   The protagonist cannot share her complex fears regarding
her quest for the father and the resurgence of memory within
herself; she fears that she will cry and "that would be horrible,
none of them would know what to do and neither would I" (15).
Her isolation from her own emotions seems peculiar, but her
isolation seems even stranger since Joe, one of the company,
is her present lover.   Joe prefers stoicism, if not apathy, to
shared emotion: ". . . he'd prefer it if I kept from showing any

reaction, no matter what has happened" (33).

For all the representatives of this generation, excepting the Surfacer, emotional links seem vestigial and suspect. Therefore, her sense of historical time, of familial responsibility, and of personal history isolates her from her peers.

On this island, she sees herself, Joe, Anna, and David as divided people, each isolated and imperilled by such separation. The Surfacer begins part two of her quest, having reluctantly entered the lake for the first time, with this key internal monologue:

> The trouble is all in the knob at the top of our bodies,
> I'm not against the body or the head either; only the
> neck which creates the illusion that they are separate. (91)

Body and mind seem often to function separately or even at cross purposes; this split promotes a body-as-object attitude. Without the neck, the Surfacer muses, humans "wouldn't be able to look down at their bodies and move them around as if they were robots or puppets; they would have to recognize that if the head is detached from the body, both of them will die" (91). This simple assessment is unsettling, but this is no new perception. Although the protagonist lacks the vocabulary, she apprehends her Cartesian dichotomy, her "dissociated sensibility." This echoes Iris Murdoch's *A Severed Head* or Eliot's "Love Song of J. Alfred Prufrock." The Surfacer uses the metaphor of the woman "sawn apart in a wooden crate, wearing a bathing suit, smiling a trick done with mirrors" (129). But Ethan Brand's unmelted heart, Kurtz's "horror," or Prufrock's "ragged claws" are simply different, powerful literary metaphors for the same perception of division. Hand functions without heart; the body functions but does not feel.

The protagonist recognizes in her peers and in herself the dangers of this divided self; she feels half alive, half formed:

> The other half, the one locked away, was the only one
> that could live; I was the wrong half, detached, terminal.
> I was nothing but a head, or, no, something minor like a
> severed thumb. numb. (129)

The Surfacer's references to body as "robot" is central to Atwood's diagnosis of this age-old dilemma of the divided sensibility. The contemporary metaphor for this is, in *Surfacing,* mechanical. Of these four adults, Atwood selects David and Anna, the married couple, to represent this dangerous, common division. All the images surrounding them are mechanical; by novel's end, both of them become, in fact, sexual robots. These are the casualties of the urban, technological society. While Joe certainly needs healing, he is not yet mechanical: "He's like the buffalo on the U. S. nickel, shaggy and blunt-snouted" (10). He can still feel; the human animal in Joe is not yet iron.

But for David and for Anna, spiritual and emotional renewal on this island proves impossible; they cannot even conceive of such connection. To examine these two as a married unit and as single individuals may clarify how Atwood dissects the contemporary dilemma for each of the sexes, or to preserve the metaphor, dismantles the nuts and bolts of our awesome, robot identities.

In her quest for identity on its emotional level, the Surfacer looks to Anna and David for knowledge. She considers them, initially, to be "the perfect couple," an awesome burden to place upon *any* two people, to be sure. But the Surfacer assumes that because David and Anna have been married for nine years (the exact time it has taken her to experience a rending affair and a haunting abortion), they "must have a special method, formula" (46). She wants from them the secret of a happy marriage, "some knowledge I missed out on" (46). Ten days of isolation, ten days in this natural world reveal a "special method" indeed.

Their method involves, unfortunately, a sado-masochism rivaled only by characters in an Albee play. While less articulate than Martha and George, Anna and David manage to annihilate one another's peace quite as effectively. Anna eventually discloses that David has, in fact, "this little set of rules."

> If I break one of them I get punished, except he keeps
> changing them so I'm never sure. (145)

Anna even suspects that David's delight in punishing her and making her cry hinges on the fact that "he can't do it himself" (145).

Yet Anna fears *losing* David almost as much as she fears

him. Her identity is fused with his, fulfilling not the promise but the peril of the romantic notion that two shall become one. Anna, in the continuing battle of the sexes which she wages with David, teaches the Surfacer about emotional desperation.

> . . . her body was her only weapon and she was fighting
> for her life, he was her life, her life was the fight . . . (180)

Anna defers to whatever David commands (wishes). An early scene, during the car journey into "foreign territory," foreshadows the regime between Anna and David. Her self-abnegation is made apparent, but the reader—quite like the narrator—is prepared to dismiss the incident. Anna begins singing in earnest: "David turned on the radio, he couldn't get anything, we were between stations. When she was in the middle of 'St. Louis Blues' he began to whistle and she stopped" (12). Characteristically, the narrator simply records this; she deduces nothing from the incident.

Nevertheless, this is not simply a case of two people's abrogating their Rogers/Astaire privileges when in company. David may suppress her simply to save her self-embarrassment, but the action, even if well-intended, blocks Anna's life sounds. These two act out the war between the sexes, seventies-style. Fear dominates them. Anna and David fail to attain the fairy-tale, social promise of "living happily" even for nine years, much less for the mythical "ever after."

Identities centered on the romantic illusion are, in Atwood's works, dysfunctional. She insists that:

> . . . the Cinderella story is somehow no longer believeable.
> We just can't believe any more that Prince Charming is
> going to solve all the problems. That has something to
> do with the nature of literature at this moment.[15]

Atwood's *The Edible Woman* (1970) presents a comic look at this dysfunction. The well-educated bride-to-be finds herself confronted by a real set of identity problems. To enjoy the fruits of the romantic illusion—prince and castle and happily ever after—she must abrogate her former self. The romantic illusion does not nourish her; it consumes her. In a fine and hilarious scene, she bakes a princess cake and disposes of the romantic identity by eating this simple, harmless embodiment of it.

In *Surfacing*, however, the princess and prince appear as anything but comic. Characters (male and female) who assume these identities regularly appear in Atwood's compositions. Readers familiar with Atwood's poetry volumes recognize, even expect, figures from fairyland. *Circle Game* employs dwarf and maiden while "The Green Giant Murder" uses exactly that. Atwood insists, in discussing the use of such figures in her *Power Politics* volume, that "myths such as Bluebeard, Dracula, and horror comic material" can actually "project certain images of men and women."[16]

Atwood examines David as the fairytale king and Anna as the fairytale princess, reinforcing this by integrating the general fairytale expectation/identity into the Surfacer's work. She brings to the island her latest commission, which involves illustrating a volume of fairytales. Her attempts to depict the perfect princess prove unsuccessful; the Surfacer admits "it isn't my territory" (62).

For her employer, Mr. Percival, and for the buying public, these fairytale figures must be "elegant and stylized, decoratively colored, like pastisserie cakes" (61). She is forbidden, for fiscal reasons, the color red; thus, color can do little to heighten the emotional quality of the story or to symbolize event or character. For this "tale of the Golden Phoenix," Mr. Percival demands "a cool tone;" she is allowed yellow. By drawing the princess her employer envisions and by having sufficient skill to distinguish golden phoenix from yellow flame from flaxen-haired princess, this commercial artist succeeds. But she wonders inside: "What's the alternative to princesses, what else will parents buy for their children? Humanoid bears and talking pigs, Protestant choo-choo trains who make the grade and become successful" (66).

But, unlike the Surfacer, Anna has identified with the fairytale princess and has faced adulthood believing the romantic illusion. Anna enters the cabin while the Surfacer attempts another "ordinary princess" complete with "emaciated fashion-model torso and infantile face" (62). Anna confides that she believed in these early models of female destiny: "I did, I thought I was really a princess and I'd end up living in a castle" (67). Her next remark and her action deepen her characteri-

zation, and disclose the enormous disillusionment which Anna
has experienced:

> "They shouldn't let kids have stuff like that."   She
> goes to the mirror, blots and smooths her face. . . (67)

In *Surfacing*, Anna represents the female who embraces
whole-heartedly the fairytale promise of the kiss, prince, timeless joy.   Yet she lives in time and must confront herself not
as the princess but as the aging queen.   In a life-long,
self-haunting game of "mirror, mirror," Anna is victimized by
her own socially-inculcated narcissism.   By accepting stereotyped models of female identity, Anna must accept the fears
and self-revulsion which they inspire. The Surfacer reluctantly
admits that cosmetics represent "the only magic left Anna"
and that she is, indeed, "the captive princess in someone's
head" (194).

In her account of Anna, Gloria Onley finds her "locked
into her Playboy centerfold stereotype, her soul trapped in a
gold   compact,   her   capacity   for   love   locked   into   a
sado-masochistic pattern."[17]   Anna is indeed caught between
princess and pin-up; by novel's end, she has learned nothing
from her return to the natural world:

> From her handbag she takes a round gilt compact with
> violets on the cover. She opens it, unclosing her other
> self, and runs her fingertips around the corners of her
> mouth . . then she unswivels a pink stick and dots her
> cheeks and blends them, changing her shape, performing
> the only magic left to her. (194)

Note that her transformation does not involve entering into
the natural world; her appearance is artificial.

Nor does David, as the prince, fare well with his identity.
He, too, feels locked into the romantic illusion and disappointed
with his role. While attempting what he considers the mandatory
seduction of the Surfacer, David reveals himself, but not quite
as he'd hoped:

> I'm all for equality of women; she [Anna] just doesn't
> happen to be equal, and that's not my fault is it? What

I married was a pair of boobs, she manipulated me. . .
(163)

And the Surfacer correctly assesses David's attempted seduction as oddly impersonal; mechanical images characterize his dissociated sensibility:

> Geometrical sex, he need me for an abstract principle; it would be enough for him if our genitals could be detached like two kitchen appliances and copulate in mid-air, that would complete his equation. (178)

This prince is barely in control of himself and manifests none of the finer qualities which occur to the Surfacer as being regal or responsible. Neither her brother nor David nor the "Americans" rule their dominion in a kingly manner. The Surfacer recalls tales in which the hero must listen to the animals and pacify their needs. As Bettelheim asserts, such actions further "self-actualization within himself and also in the world."[18] As fairytale king, David is deaf to the living creatures and can neither receive guidance nor give protection.

Nor does he positively represent the fairytale hunter who, as Bettelheim states, subdues his own "violent tendencies" and uses the power to kill or capture for benevolent purposes.[19] David does not preserve and defend life, as the fairytale hunter must. David hunts not with a gun but with a camera; to clarify the correlations between hunter/photographer in *Surfacing* is to clarify not only characterization but also a major symbol: the camera.

As David's "Random Samples" testifies, dominance over the natural world supplants cooperation. The ties between animals and human animals seem frayed, if not entirely severed. The narrator laments such separation:

> The king who learned to speak with animals, in the story he ate a magic leaf and they revealed a treasure, a conspiracy, they saved his life; what would they really say? Accusation, lament, an outcry of rage; but they had no spokesman. (154)

This is no land of princesses; this is not a time of benevolent kings.

Failures as princess and prince, Anna and David attempt the adult correlatives: pin-up "girl" and play "boy." Thus, Anna stars in her husband's deadly and pornographic home-movie. While oblivious to how horrific the images filmed actually are, she is sufficiently perceptive—or antagonistic—to call the pretentious exercise "Random Pimples." David insists that she disrobe for the movie; he mocks her:

> You'll go in beside the dead bird, it's your chance for
> stardom, you've always wanted fame. You'll get to be
> on Educational TV. . . (158)

His dangerous, socially-imbued desire to be a playboy, a photographer of nude women, has not abated over the years. His woman-as-object attitude has eaten something essential and human away, as acid might. His whole world view is afflicted; note this revelatory comment on his Communications course which he teaches at an adult education center:

> ". . . maybe I'll make it a short course this time," David
> said. "For the businessman on how to open the *Playboy*
> centerfold with the left hand only, keeping the right free
> for action. ." (133)

Nor is his opinion of women any higher than his opinion of men, whom he fancies share his puerile obsession: ". . . for the housewives how to switch on TV and switch off their heads, that's all they need to know, then we can go home" (133).

For these and other remarks, Anna calls David a "woman-hater," yet his problem—while as insidious—is more inclusive. David suffers what the Surfacer calls "an atrophy of the heart." David loves nothing alive. Yet he considers himself, in a phrase which would surely rankle Leonardo d'Vinci or Jacob Bronowski, one of the "new Renaissance Men" (12). David understands nothing of renascence; he chooses for his film only images of decay, death, devastation: stuffed moose dressed in human clothing, rotting heron, dismembered trees. David represents not the second-coming of the Quattrocento sensibility but, unsettlingly enough, "the second-hand American."

David's "Random Samples" records his response to the

natural world; his directoral eye is deadly indeed. This eschatological document indicts the mechanical Adam, the metallic
male. In accepting the identities offered to adults by glossy,
sex magazines which are considered chic, David and Anna represent the pornographic inversion of the romantic identity.

Their sensibilities are not dissociated but severed. As
representatives of a generation experiencing "Love without
fear, sex without risk" (96), they manifest a frightening
emotional paralysis. Anna in her compact and David with his
camera embody the worst aspects of impersonal, urban, sex-
related existence. These two stand as the old centerfold; they
are a tin bride/groom statue on a welded wedding cake. Anna
represents what Kate Millet's *Sexual Politics* analyzes as "the
familiar triad" which oppresses and defines the female; passivity,
masochism, and narcissism. David, of course, represents the
devastating male triad which oppresses and defines that sex:
dominance, sadism, and meglomania.

In their failure to connect mind and heart, personal and
cultural history, David and Anna refuse adulthood. Any
personal, ethical, complete identity seems beyond their imaginations. They are commercial identities, products of fairytale images and pre-packaged sex concepts. In fine, they represent a generation threatened with emotional extinction:
"The machine is gradual," the Surfacer understands, "it takes
a little of you at a time, it leaves the shell" (195). This she
learns from perceiving Anna and David, from discarding the
metallic barriers which she herself has accumulated.

Thus, David and Anna do more than represent some
reductive example of the wearisome "perfect couple." Their
fear of time partially explains their mutual/individual desire
to escape from personal and cultural history. David and Anna
wish to escape from absolutes, but time, like emotional history,
proves inescapable. Fear is not transcendence. Nevertheless,
Anna lives in her ruling object, her compact, and worries each
wrinkle into place. David combs his thinning hair in bangs,
signalling his premature baldness. Both fear the aging process,
considering it unnatural. In the youth culture created by contemporary, western technological society, this fear is inculcated.

They represent the dysfunction of sexual identities. The
Surfacer's final assessment of David and Anna reflects no hope
for their reunification of mind and body. The mechanical male

and the mechanical female are mere performers in their own pornographic productions. Even in the act of love—or, as they would surely call it—the sex act, David and Anna are not alive:

> She copulates under strobe lights with the man's torso
> while his brain watches from its glassed-in cubicle at
> the other end of the room, her face twists in poses of
> exultation and abandon, that is all. (195)

"Pose" replaces authentic feeling and movement just as the playboy/pin-up illusions replace identity.

That David and Anna are not aberrants but are, rather, microcosmic representatives of our technological generation must not be overlooked. Through them, a reexamination of modern division within the self and between the sexes proves illuminating. This princess/pin-up and the prince/playboy are sad, of course, but are also awesome and dangerous. They are victims and victimizers; becoming more and more static in their perceptions of existence, they cannot discern the natural from the artificial, the life-giving from the death-dealing. Body-as-object does, indeed, produce emotionally irresponsible men and women; David and Anna are sexual mechanics. No more.

And in the Surfacer's refusal to turn away from these difficult lessons, in her ability to face disappointment in her hopes for having discovered "the perfect couple," she brings her generation closer to connecting the mind/heart. She burns the glossy female identities; she unravels the film in those "re-demptive" waters. Rediscovery of the natural human, for Atwood, seems a perilous ascent but a necessary one. Further mechanization of our species seems unthinkable. In her scrutiny of our sexual patterns, our generational tensions, and our human identities, Atwood proclaims our perils and our possibilities in a steady, a necessary voice.

Atwood's protagonist must examine her identity against these sexual and generational patterns which she perceives in the microcosm. Her hope for connection with the natural world and with emotional wholeness helps her to understand why Joe, her taciturn and passive companion, is a much less dangerous male than prince David. While David and Anna find mechanical images with which to identify, Joe and the Surfacer do not. Atwood carefully maintains Joe's symbol in the natural world.

The Surfacer ponders another kind of fairy/folk tale called "loup-garou." In such tales, the Surfacer recalls, "the animals are human inside and they take their fur skins off as easily as getting undressed" (65). This process also works in the reverse. Joe seems just such a figure; the narrator surrounds him with animal images. He "unzips his skin" upon retiring (189). The narrator trusts him precisely because he seems animal and is not yet mechanical, as are David and Anna.

> . . . he's like the buffalo on the U. S. nickel, shaggy and
> blunt-snouted, with small clenched eyes and the defiant
> but insane look of a species once dominant, now threat-
> ened with extinction. (10)

His hairy physicality and his non-verbal ways bring simple body comfort to the narrator. The human animal in Joe seems still capable of emotion.

Her attraction to shaggy Joe and her preference for animal stories also indicate her abiding, animistic imagination. While princesses and princes stir little awe or belief, the narrator finds transformation from beast to human or vice versa profound and miraculous. This fascination guides the ways in which she perceives the living and the dead. Such transformations, in fact, seem a salient feature of Atwood's works. She seems interested in such protean changes; asked about "evolutionary changes" in an interview, Atwood reveals the early and fruitful influence of myth and story:[20]

> . . . most fairytales and religious stories involve changes
> of shape. Grimm's tales, Greek and Celtic legends, have
> them. North American Indian legends have people who
> are animals in one incarnation, and who can take on the
> shape of a bird at will.

The Surfacer thinks she sees her father's "wolf's eyes," and she identifies her mother with bluejays. She feels akin to the heron and perceives Joe as the buffalo. In an astute review of *Circle Game* for *Nation*, Rosellen Brown notes the "primitive vision" that informs Atwood's works: "The animals are totems," Brown asserts, "things pass from one form to another easily."[21] Animism manifest by this Surfacer is, on one hand, distinctly marked by the Indian tradition so influential in the Canadian consciousness.*   This sense of nature in its "Manitou" power prepares the protagonist for her shamanistic initiation in Part III.

Note in the fishing expedition with Joe, David, and Anna, for example, how the Surfacer concentrates on the act. (One of the interesting inversions in this novel, of course, is that this woman is familiar with survival techniques; the males and Anna have no such knowledge.) The Surfacer distinguishes between her hunting techniques and her brother's:

> I stare into the water, it was always a kind of meditation.
> My brother fished by techniques, he outguessed them, but
> I fished by prayer, listening. . . He got more fish but I
> could pretend mine were willing, they had chosen to
> die and forgiven me in advance. (74)

This animism is further supported by her understanding of familiar fairytales.   Bruno Bettelheim analyses the human penchant toward animism; talking with the animals seems peculiar neither to Dr. Doolittle nor to native North Americans. Bettelheim's remarks, in fact, clarify how the Surfacer's folk tale beliefs unite human/animal, living/dead.   With animistic tendencies, he declares, "everything is inhabited by the child's projected spirit."   Since the protagonist unites her childhood and adult ideas of a Spiritus Mundi, Bettelheim's discriminations do serve to explain her.   He further stipulates in his useful study, *The Uses of Enchantment:*

> . . . because of this inherent sameness it is believable
> that man can change into animal, or the other way a-
> round. . . Since there is no sharp line drawn between
> living and dead things, the latter, too, can come to life.
> (10)

His remarks supplement rather well those of Atwood regarding

---

* Atwood devotes an entire chapter of *Survival* to this aspect of Canadian identity.

the Jamesian ghost, as projections of the self either into nature or another form.

And this belief in the spiritual connection between the human and the natural world seems essential to the examination of personal identity. Atwood's use of this concept makes *Surfacing* a novel not only about the individual woman who comes into knowledge but also about the Canadian who does so. Interestingly enough, Northrop Frye finds this Indian influence throughout the Canadian literary tradition:[22]

> . . . the Indians symbolize a primitive mythological imagination which is being reborn in us: in other words, the white Canadians, in their imaginations, are no longer immigrants but are becoming indigenous, recreating the kind of attitudes appropriate to people who really belong here.

Many critics find this sensibility distinctly opposed to what has, through the archetype of the "American Adam," become popularized as the American sensibility. This Surfacer hunts differently than, say, the hunters in Dickey's *Deliverance*; her attitude manifests an almost North American Indian relationship with the animal.

To examine identity "against" another identity, Atwood uses the term "second-hand American" which is, according to Margot Northey, a "synecdoche" for western, technological society. David, as "the second-hand American," therefore, represents "the social manifestation of a specific attitude" which, according to Northey, involves:

> . . . an excessive belief in man's rationality and his ability to dominate both his own body (by suppressing natural passion) and the world around him.[23]

To characterize the erstaz American, Atwood simply utilizes models offered by literary tradition, particularly those of Northrop Frye and of Leslie Fiedler. Frye stipulates that the extroverted violence in the United States contrasts with the introverted violence in Canada. That is, the Canadian literary

tradition condemns the wanton subjugation of the natural
world.*   Leslie Fiedler, in his analysis of the United States
literary tradition, proclaims an exuberance for the male test
which involves the subjugation of nature.

Atwood cites Fiedler's *Love and Death in the American
Novel* during an interview with the *Chicago Review:*[24]

> In American literature you killed the animal and achieved
> something by doing it; in the Canadian one, you killed
> the animal and it was a negative achievement.

Like the apotheosized American Adam, then, David exults
in conquest; he delights in dominating the natural world. For
example, when finding the mutilated heron, the protagonist
is deeply revulsed, but David responds excitedly. His director's
eye is deadly, indeed; another eschatological image enters "Random Samples" which seems an increasingly sinister documentary:

> "We need that," David said, "we can put it next to the
> fish guts."
>
> "Shit," Joe said, "it really stinks."
>
> "That won't show in the movie," David said, "you can
> stand it for five minutes, it looks so great, you have to
> admit it." (138)

David belongs to the male ethos celebrated in *Deliverance.*
Criticism of *Surfacing,* in fact, often parallels these two
novels. The most illuminating of these articles is by Rosemary
Sullivan. She quotes James Dickey, himself, and examines both
works as diametrical opposites which represent the Canadian/
American, female/male ethos. Quite simply, Sullivan uses
Surfacing and *Deliverance* to indicate value difference between
the American Eve and the American Adam. Sullivan finds

---

* Frye's analysis of this literary position informs all of his critical
works; *The Bushe Garden* (1971) develops the theory.

Dickey's archetypal male characters fixated by a nostalgia for the test of violence and bent on the subjugation of nature. This male, in turn, believes that nature is hostile and bent upon his destruction.

As Dickey rather sweepingly remarks: "There's a God-like feeling about fighting on our planet." Sullivan notes his novel's romanticization of this attitude:[25]

> Dickey has made self-conscious the lure of violence which is endemic to American romanticism, but he is honest with himself when he draws no moral revulsion from this.

Among such archetypal American characters, nature is a battle-ground; the war against nature marches beside the battle of the sexes. Atwood's *Survival* thus summarizes the Adamic attitude:[26]

> The war against Nature assumed that Nature was hostile to begin with; man could fight and lose, or he could fight and win. If he won he would be rewarded: he could conquer and enslave Nature and in practical terms, exploit her resources.

In *Surfacing* David embodies these ideas toward nature; David and Anna personify the sexual battles. For many critics, *Surfacing* repudiates "power-lust and violence."[27] Sullivan finds the Canadian novel, in general, and Atwood's novel, in particular, a literary force which "insists on the need to move beyond the predator-pursued, killer-victim mentality." This new vision and commitment, according to Sullivan, recognizes "a sacrificial cycle of life dying to sustain life." Thus, the human (male/female) in nature "is not hunter but supplicant and the energy he absorbs from nature is not that of power but of awe, the capacity of worship."[28] Clearly, these Canadian critics reflect the pacific, kindred attitude toward the natural world reminiscent of native values.

If the mythic archetype in America seems a male ethos driven, as Fiedler asserts, toward dominance, then the mythic archetype in Canada seems a female ethos, driven—as Frye stipulates—toward "a nostalgia for a world of peace"[29] and dominated by a pastoral myth distinctly different from that celebrated in this nation's literature.

Water becomes the symbolic element for that peaceful unification. In Atwood's *Surfacing,* water is the medium of purification and rebirth. Her brother, a Phlebas/Lazarus figure, communicates no transforming knowledge. The Surfacer, conversely, returns from that foreign and familiar element with knowledge. Perhaps Atwood connects water with the Canadian identity, too, because she mentions in The *American Poetry Review* that:

> Water is important in my work because if you look at
> an aerial map of Canada, you will see that there is more
> water per square mile there than in almost any other
> country on earth. Therefore, the key element for Canada
> is water.[30]

The Surfacer finds new language for her new knowledge; with her initiation, her stream-of-consciousness perceptions seem at once diffuse and unifying. She transmogrifies into nature; she is human, animal, tree, place. "Everything," she wonders, "is made of water."

> In one of the languages there are no nouns, only verbs
> held for a longer moment.
>   The animals have no need for speech, why talk when
> you are a word
>   I lean against a tree, I am a tree leaning.

Through such chaotic association rises, again, her animistic imagination.

She does, in her fashion, tell all. The "gift of feeling" exchanges itself with the "true vision" which attends "the failure of logic." Roughly translated, she unites feeling and thought, reason and vision. She judges her life's actions, accepts knowledge of and responsibility for nothing less than good and evil. She knows that her parents gifted her with a preference for life (220). She determines to act upon that preference, which—given the world view recorded on "Random Samples"—seems no simple resolve. She faces personal history; she effaces "false memory" which she created because, in her words: "I couldn't accept it, that ruin I'd made" (169). While she admits the faked album of memory, she admits, too that "a paper house was better than none and I could almost live in it, I'd lived in it until now" (169). "Almost" live remains the unsettling qualifier; by accepting real action and ethical responsibility, she can attempt "to trust and let go" (224). Such letting go involves self trust which, upon refusing "to be a victim," the Surfacer establishes.

The Surfacer becomes, then, not only the embodiment of the Canadian sensibility but also of the natural woman. She casts off the detritus of the romantic illusion and its *Playboy* perversion.

The Surfacer, conversely, is "a new kind of centerfold;" this woman-in-nature looks nothing like the imitation woman. After her three day initiation into human identity, "a tanned body on a beach with washed hair waving like scarves" (222) she assuredly is not. Rather, her face is earth-smeared and her hair resembles "a frayed bathmat stuck with leaves and twigs" (222). This strange centerfold looks nothing like a princess, not even an Indian one. She seems, herself, a creature from a "loup garou" story.

Nameless and questing, the Surfacer has transmogrified and returned to human form. She seems an archetype indeed: a hero, but not one who revels in violence. She encounters peril; she attains knowledge and never kills anything but fear. The journey leads physically outward, metaphysically inward as must all heroic passages. Although I am inclined to see her as a specifically Conradian hero, the traditional apparatus of all heroic initiation informs *Surfacing*.

Perhaps the character's very namelessness suggests a pilgrim's progress, an Everyone's or Everywoman's quest. And if the universal attends "her," then her nameless family, too— father, mother, brother—take on dimensions of archetype. Two fine articles already quoted adequately trace "the lineaments of myth" which George Woodcock senses in *Surfacing*. Rosemary Sullivan utilizes the heroic process outlined by Mircea Eliade's *Rites and Symbols of Initiation*; J. P. Campbell's "The Woman as Hero in *Surfacing*" uses the formula outlined in Joseph Campbell's *The Hero of a Thousand Faces*. The novel's progress includes the journey, the testing, the descent/ascent, the transformation through knowledge, and the return.

A true hero, the Surfacer must return; interestingly, her decision to do so has spurred controversy among readers and critics. Some reject her decision to create a relationship with Joe; others find her creating a child an anti-abortion position. She believes the "seed of death" has been planted in her by that early abortion; given her belief structure—which she becomes aware of in this island awakening—her actions seem entirely *in character*. Still, the controversy seems to me a testament to good literature; also, Atwood, it seems, has constructed a character at once archetypal and singular. The hero is at once Everywoman and one particular human entity who must resolve not to imitate emotion or belief or identity. This commitment seems essential to a novel which explores the individual coming into knowledge: the person acting "con-scientia."

This first-person narrator seems to me the greatest technical risk and achievement in Atwood's novel. To examine the crucial issues of isolation, identity, integration, Atwood constructs as first-person narrator an inveterate liar, or, at least, a self-deceiver. This narrator *becomes* reliable. She becomes responsible for, quite simply, her true life's story. The narrator's intricate self-delusion unravels quite subtly; until the Surfacer's ascent from the lake, in fact, a good reader might overlook the small discrepancies which attend the narrator's repeated, slightly varied recollections of the "aborted" husband and child.

Atwood intended, apparently, some shock of recognition in the reader. "The reader who endorses the character," she remarks, "suddenly finds out she's been telling horrible lies."[31] By creating a character whose encounters in adult life have been so self-alienating that she creates false memories, the author prevents too facile an identification with the protagonist. We are at once she and not she, as it were. Thus, who the Surfacer indeed *is* is as much part of the mystery/quest as the fate of the missing father. Yet so solidly is the foundation set between narrator and reader that even her shocking self-revelations and shamanistic initiation are supported.

This success attests Atwood's considerable skill with the stream-of-consciousness narrative. As with most stream-of-consciousness novels, associative logic constructs the islands in that stream. These islands are perceptual units within the character or external events which reveal her and other characters. Atwood uses scenes like the discovery of the mutilated heron or Anna's forced disrobing, as I've indicated, to compare/contrast the Surfacer's perceptions with those of the other characters.   Her sometimes eerie, dispassionate objectivity, juxtaposed with her awakening emotional understanding which is quite subjective, helps characterize her.   This establishes, too, the divisions extant between her internal values and her external actions.   She must, as her interior monologue reveals, heal herself.

The narrator's constant internal monologue gives the reader intimate information; the reader understands many conflicts before the character does.   What she thinks and how she thinks provide a basis of credibility between reader and character.   Many of her recollections seem accurate, perceptive: history class we remember and communion within the natural world, the child's space.   With self-scrutiny, she exposes the human need for such strenuous responsibility.   She knows that, to avoid the same static identities that mechanize Anna and David, she must not confuse a description of reality (via *Playboy* or fairy tale or *Vogue*) with reality itself.   To do so violates body and mind, feeling and consideration.

Surfacing is essentially a novel about contemporary identity and the quest for unity.   The protagonist must connect her intellectual and emotional aspects; she must connect her past and present.   The Surfacer must affirm the links between herself and her parents, understanding the values of the male and of the female.   On a spiritual level, the Surfacer seeks the unification of the female and male aspects of divinity.

That many critics consider this a novel of a woman's spiritual quest is understandable.*   But this quest for spiritual integration connects the female to the social plane.   Atwood's hero surfaces, and she accepts the world as her own responsibility.   She creates her world daily.   The Surfacer refuses, therefore, the complicity of passivity; she rejects woman as victim much as Canada must refuse the submergence of its values and identities in those of the United States.

---

* Carol P. Christ's "Margaret Atwood: The Surfacing of Woman's Spiritual Quest and Vision," (*Signs* 2, No. 2, 1976) explores this issue and provides a concise explanation of the problem.

This renascence in Canadian consciousness is, according to Northrop Frye, an affirmation of "a future in which modern man has come home from his exile in the land of unlikeness and has become something better than the ghost of an ego haunting himself."[32] In its refusal to romanticize Existential angst, to apotheosize the "second-hand American identity," or to endorse the dangerous identities of princess and playboy, *Surfacing* announces a movement away from the self-haunting and self-deluding hero.

This new scrutiny involves issues old and new: ecology, sexual politics, planetary consciousness, individuality, and ethical self-rule. Atwood, in turn, employs "ironic modification" to illuminate these issues, re-analyzing our stereotypic princess and prince. If *Surfacing* is, indeed, a consummately modern and Canadian novel, theirs seems a literature which may help the unification of the North American sensibility. As ever, such knowledge must prove transfiguring.

Notes

[1] Claude Bissell, "Politics and Literature in the 1960's," *Literary History of Canada*, ed. Carl F. Klinck, 2nd, ed., III (Toronto: University of Toronto Press, 1976), p. 15. Ronald Sutherland's *Second Image* (1971) critical connection of French and English literary traditions in Canada remains a seminal work.

[2] Desmond Pacey, "The Course of Canadian Criticism," *Literary History of Canada*, p. 26.

[3] Ellen Coughlin, "Margaret Atwood," *Books and Arts,* 7 March 80, pp. 5-6.

[4] George Woodcock, "Margaret Atwood as Novelist," *The Canadian Novel in the Twentieth Century*, ed. George Woodcock, (Toronto: McClelland & Steward Ltd., 1975), p. 327.

[5] Northrop Frye, "Conclusion," *Literary History of Canada*: Canadian Literature in English, 2nd ed., ed. Carl F. Klinck, III (Toronto: University of Toronto Press, 1976), p. 321.

[6]Northrop Frye, "Conclusion," *Literary History of Canada*, 2nd ed., ed. Carl F. Klinck, III, p. 324.

[7]Frye, "Conclusion," p. 324.

[8]Frye, "Conclusion," p. 321.

[9]Margaret Atwood, *Surfacing*, (New York: Popular Library, 1976), p. 14. All citations taken from this text.

[10]Northrop Frye, *Anatomy of Criticism: Four Essays* (Princeton: Princeton University Press, 1957), p. 203.

[11]Northrop Frye, *The Bushe Garden* (Toronto: Anansi Publishers, 1971), p. 239.

[12]Margot Northey, *The Haunted Wilderness: The Gothic And Grotesque in Canadian Fiction* (Toronto: University of Toronto Press, 1976), p. 67.

[13]Josie P. Campbell, "The Woman as Hero in Margaret Atwood's *Surfacing,"* *Mosaic*, XI, 3, (1978), pp. 17-28.

[14]Linda Sandler, "Interview with Margaret Atwood," *The Malahat Review*, 41, January (1977), pp. 7-27.

[15]Ellen Coughlin, "Margaret Atwood," *Books and Arts,* 7 March 80, p. 6.

[16]Sandler, Ibid., p. 10.

[17]Gloria Onley, "Power Politics in Bluebeard's Castle," *Canadian Literature*, 60, Spring (1974), p. 26.

[18]Bruno Bettelheim, *The Uses of Enchantment* (New York: Vintage Books, 1977), p. 102.

[19]Bettelheim, p. 177.

[20]Sandler, Ibid., p. 14.

[21]Rosellen Brown, "Review: *Circle Game,"* *Nation*, 212, (1971), pp. 824-26.

[22]Northrop Frye, "Haunted by Lack of Ghosts," *The Canadian Imagination*, ed. David Staines (Cambridge: Harvard University Press, 1977), p. 40.

[23]Northey, p. 66.

[24]Mary Ellis Gibson, "A Conversation with Margaret Atwood," *Chicago Review*, Vol. 27 (1976), p. 109.

[25]Rosemary Sullivan, *Surfacing and Deliverance,"* *Canadian Literature*, 67, Winter (1976), p. 12.

[26]Margaret Atwood, *Survival* (Toronto: House of Anansi Press, 1972), p. 60.

[27]Tom Marshall, "Atwood Under and Above Water," *The Malahat Review*, 41 (1977), p. 90.

[28]Sullivan, p. 13.

[29]Northrop Frye, *The Bushe Garden* (Toronto: House of Anansi, 1971), p. 239.

[30]Karla Hammond, "An Interview with Margaret Atwood, *"The* *American Poetry Review,* 8, No. 5, pp. 27-29.

[31]Sandler, Ibid., p. 17.

[32]Northrop Frye, "Haunted by Lack of Ghosts," *The Canadian Imagination,* ed. David Staines (Cambridge: Harvard University Press, 1977), p. 45.

Love and Aging: Lessing and the Female Exile

Because of Doris Lessing's considerable reputation as an innovative and experimental novelist, this short, conventional work, *The Summer Before the Dark,* seems an arresting anomaly. It does not, as does the *Children of Violence* series,* examine the major social forces of our century; it examines neither place nor person with true epic reach or intensity. This is not, certainly, the masterwork to place Lessing in the august company of, say, a Dorothy Richardson (*Pilgrimage*) or a Marcel Proust.

The Summer Before the Dark is hardly as narratively daring as *Briefing for a Descent into Hell,* wherein Charles Watkins is either quite mad or the only sane voice in an irrational place. *The Summer Before the Dark* is not as structurally experimental as *The Golden Notebook,* not as prophetic as *Memoirs of a Survivor,* not as futuristic as the *Canopus in Argos: Archives* series.

Nevertheless, this conventional novel warrants the attention these other works receive. Succinct and complex, *The Summer Before the Dark* encapsulates the major themes and salient techniques of Doris Lessing. As such, it serves as a "Reader's Guide" through Lessing's formidable literary terrain. Hers are penumbral regions of reality and self-delusion, of darkness and illumination through which, at once terrified and inspired, her exact and exacting characters tentatively grope and dance. Lessing's protagonists, by exploring language and memory and dream, discover self. They confront what Martha Quest calls "the dragons" which are, quite simply, the fears which regulate human behavior:

> . . . fear of what other people think, fear of being dif-

---

* *Martha Quest, A Proper Marriage, A Ripple from the Storm, Landlocked,* and *The Four-Gated City* comprise her famous pentology.

> ferent, fear of being isolated, fear of the herd we belong
> to, fear of that part of the herd we belong to.[1]

The "dragons" are both personally and socially created; they defend the status quo and guard the sanctuaries of self-knowledge. Despite their terrors, protagonists in Lessing's novels confront these dragons.

Kate Brown, the protagonist of *The Summer Before the Dark,* is as conventional as the novel itself. Kate Brown's scrupulous conformity makes her admissions of frustration and of self-delusion startling. Hardly a life-long non-conformist and seeker as is the illustrious Martha Quest, Kate Brown nevertheless assails her dragons. This intelligent, decorous matron—for whom husband, children, home have sufficed—begins a journey into disturbing self-knowledge which calls into question her motives and achievements.

Yet the novel's beginning hardly presages a perilous adventure.

> A woman stood on her back step, arms folded, waiting.[2]

Her venture promises to be less fantastic than domestic. Yet this, the shortest chapter, proves the first and last time this woman stands on her own ground; a journey awaits. In this fine and ironic first chapter, Lessing establishes the protagonist as individual and as archetype. She recreates the fabled exile from the garden, with contemporary irony.

For example, when focusing on the experiences of aging, marriage, or motherhood, Lessing employs the refrain "a woman" to widen the focus. This one woman thus represents her entire gender. She is nameless but recognizable; she is a housewife: "a pretty, healthy, serviceable woman" (7). Her deliberations and subsequent actions establish character and conflicts. "A woman," the narrator repeats, "stood on her back doorstep, arms folded, waiting for a kettle to boil" (1). These are modern times, but she boils water over an outdoor fire because of a contemporary problem: power failure. This metaphor of modern life initiates the action; this old chore assumes timely and timeless dimensions, around which the novel moves.

"A woman" waits that she may prepare the coffee for

her husband and his guest. She seems quite the Miltonian ideal: she waits *and* serves.*

> A woman, as she might have done any time during the
> past several hundred years, stood under a tree, holding
> a crowded tray. (7)

And, like Milton's Eve, she must be banished; in a garden, beneath a tree: the archetype rises almost effortlessly. But this Eve, her hands safely full, does not consciously seek knowledge, although unsettling questions keep intruding upon her consciousness. She does not withhold obedience to husband or household chores, although such matters seem less satisfying of late. Despite her passivity, knowledge of good and evil and exile activate her.

After serving with pleasure, "a woman" settles down to enjoy her own coffee, careful to "set an attentive smile on her face, like a sentinel, behind which she could cultivate her own thoughts" (11). Ever vigilant and responsive to the needs of others and to the commands of others, she deliberates summer management of her household—the arrivals and departures of husband and grown children, all mobile. Such decisions prove futile; her life for this summer is decided for her by her husband and his quest. They move her from family service into business service; she must leave beautiful house and garden. She begins a journey into knowledge.

And as with all Lessing's protagonists, new knowledge begins with an examination of language. While waiting in her garden, in fact, Kate Brown reviews the phrases which comprise the social language:

> She was letting words and phrases worn as nursery rhymes
> slide around her tongue, for towards the crucial experi-
> ences, custom allots certain attitudes and they are pretty
> stereotyped. (1)

---

* *The Return of Eden* by Northrop Frye contains this statement: "And when Eve serves the meal, goes away, and leaves the men to their masculine conversation, we feel that we are as close as Paradise can get to port and cigars," p. 66.

That she hears such language as childish rhyme presages her discoveries; her identity, too, proves to be premised on childish tales and expectations. Kate Brown's dissatisfaction with social diction initiates self-scrutiny because she is, by her own admission, fluent at "middle class verbal games" (75).

The Summer Before the Dark is, as all Lessing works are, deeply concerned with how language molds identity. She examines how language reveals and conceals our social values. In our time, this preoccupation seems shared, of course. Language seems devalued and, quite possibly, as Margaret Atwood attests in "Their Attitudes Differ," has suffered a mortal blow in our century:*

> Language, the fist proclaims by squeezing, is for the weak only.

Yet to writers like Atwood and Lessing, how the weak use language to define human experience seems important, despite the fact that money (and weapons and systems) talk.

In a dream, Anna Wulf of *The Golden Notebook* finds an archetypal image which, I suspect, illumines this concern in the writings of Doris Lessing.[3] Anna Wulf, the writer-protagonist, bears "a kind of casket" toward a group of "businessmen, brokers, something like that." They refuse to open the box; they manifest no curiosity. Rather, they press upon the writer "large sums of money." Desperate to disclose the contents, Anna opens the casque herself, exposing a "mass of fragments and pieces" which represent the contemporary world. Within are precious objects: bits of flesh from Korean War victims, clumps of raped African land, torn political badges. But the men see only "a small green crocodile with a winking, sardonic snout" at the bottom of this casque. The crocodile weeps diamonds.

For Anna Wulf, novels which open the world for the world's inspection seem dismissed as paid performances, as clever fictions. The writer, that crocodile, is perceived by established

---

* Margaret Atwood's *Power Politics* volume (New York: Simon & Schuster, 1971) employs various fairytale identities and parallels, as do her novels.

orders as amusing and profitable, perhaps, but dismissible, surely. Anna's inability to arrest attention or to alter the world through language is problematic for all Lessing's characters. And for their author. To open any Lessing novel is to unseal a Pandora's box; human ills fly forth. At the bottom of such literary causes, hope barely flickers. And that adamant hope involves a terrifying encounter with knowledge: knowledge of human fear and greed and possibility. Each is a multifaceted representation of the modern world. In Lessing's works, and for Lessing's characters, language can transform our understanding of the world. Language can, individually if not collectively, change the world. For all explorations of self, in the beginning is the Word.

Her characters' study of social language and self begins not with abstract phrases but with simple, conventional terms. Such shared phrases tap "underground rivers" for protagonists from Martha Quest to Anna Wulf to Kate Brown:

> . . . all kinds of half-buried, half-childish, myth-bred emotions were being dragged to the surface: words having such power![4]

Within shared, stale social dicta, Martha Quest finds a world to explore: "I want to take words as ordinary as bread. Or life. "Or death," she vows in *The Four-Gated City*. "I want to have my nose rubbed in cliches" (101).

Kate Brown, too, examines banalities, with less questing fervor; she fears this scrutiny. Kate Brown suspects that cliches mitigate against self-awareness. She suspects, further, that such language conspires against the expressions of true feeling. Even, she fears, these phrases infantalize us all:

> . . . it is probable that many go on repeating "Youth is the best time of your life" or "Love is a woman's whole existence" until they catch sight of themselves in a mirror while they are saying something of the kind or are quick enought to catch the reaction on a friend's face. (3)

That Kate Brown, standing in her garden and at the edge of exile, chooses these two aphorisms from the thousands available proves revelatory. Two conditions—love and age—obsess Kate Brown as she examines her life as a woman.

For both love and aging, Kate Brown admits that cliches
serve as only superficial statements. Such stock phrases seem
not only acceptable but preferable to potentially embarrassing
and possibly searing self-disclosures. Social language, in fine,
obfuscates and confines quite as easily as it clarifies and releases.
That modern protagonist, J. Alfred Prufrock, is as contemporary
as ever and not alone in recognizing that "eyes fix you in a
formulated phrase" and prevent personal declaration. Kate
Brown, too, hears social diction as little more than a "particularly efficient advertising campaign," which promotes a slick,
superficial identity. Such, decides this utterly conventional
and intelligent woman, is the social language. This "official
language" promotes not the delights and perils of individual
expression but the numbing stock of banalities which confirm
the status quo.

Such language regiments identity; memory and feeling
conform to the phrases. Nevertheless, recognitions surface
which terrify those most fluent in "official language." Aging
Mrs. Quest and Mrs. Foster of *The Four-Gated City,* for example,
sit "talking in the official language about time, life, death,"
during a sea voyage. Even with conventional phrases "knowledge gave the barest phrases a depth which made it hard sometimes for them to meet one another's eyes" (265). Kate Brown,
too, waiting for the kettle to boil, suspects the full import of
these cliches; she judged such language, however, tiresome
and ill-fitting:

> The truth was, she was becoming more and more un-
> comfortably conscious not only that the things she said,
> and a good many of the things she thought, had been
> taken down off a rack and put on, but that what she
> really felt was something else again. (2)

This investigation has attracted and repelled her for several
years. She recalls "cow sessions" (149) with her neighbor and
alter-ego, Mary Finchley, during which they have, hilariously,
scrutinized the sociological and psychological terms which
putatively define their lives. Words like "well-adjusted, typical,
normal, integrated" start the entertainment; phrases like "father
of my children" and "bread-winner" soon reduce them to tears.
The clinical sobriquet which an educational counselor applies

to Kate Brown's clan seems, during such "cow sessions," absurd to her. "Yes, a unit she said we were," Kate recalls. "Not only that, a nuclear unit" (150).

She and Mary Finchley "shriek like harpies" as terminology is reviewed.

> It was a ritual, like the stag parties of suburban men in which everything their normal lives are dedicated to upholding is spat on, insulted, belittled. (150)

But Kate Brown feels an increasing discomfort and ends these irreverent exchanges. She is, after all, centering her life's energies within that nuclear unit and fears its ridicule. The dragon, fear of language, subdues her for a time.

Without her banishment, in fact, language alone may not have sufficed to provoke Kate Brown toward self-knowledge. She longs to remain within the bonds of the family; she has felt challenged, useful, often happy within it and only unwillingly admits to herself how it devours her. She has served devotedly; she has accepted the post-Industrial definition of "a woman's" true sphere: according to this still active definition "the welfare of men and children" constitutes "the true mission of women."[5]   Kate Brown has tried to realize the familial ideal, with the female inside and the male outside the castle/home. Given her dedication, she wonders what has provoked her exile.

She has, quite simply, outlived her usefulness within this fleeting unit; she is no longer needed as full-time wife or mother. As a properly socialized, conventional female, she has expected such changes, but not so soon and not without a retirement celebration among her dispersing "nuclear unit." Kate struggles to accept this shift, admitting that "her energies must be switched from said children to less vulnerable targets, for everybody's sake . . . her own as well as theirs" (19). But her emotions defy her intelligence; she must struggle with the knowledge that she is, to both children and husband, not only dismissible but dismissed. This exile of "a woman" awaits us all because it begins, as does life some say, at forty.

Her true sphere is redefined; according to the next phase of her programming, the business world awaits her services. She wants to examine what loving and aging mean, what her experiences as a wife and as a mother have done to her who, at an attractive and lively forty-five years of age, is retired from her old identities.   Yet, her immediate and successful transition into the business world as a translator and executive with Global Food* pleases her family. Her employment relieves this loving "nuclear unit" which—she reluctantly and painfully acknowledges—maintains a vested interest in her continuing along the approved route.

It is said that pride goeth before the fall, and Kate Brown has prided herself on her efficiency within the home. Her pride suffers considerably, therefore, when her husband closes the house without discussion and with one phone call. She feels "dismissed, belittled, because the problem of the house was being considered so unimportant" (18).   To this housewife, this dismissal is a form of being flayed alive; she feels forceably retired: "With a great screaming wrench, Kate's years of conditioning for itemized responsibility ripped off her" (22). Thus exiled into business, Kate's next awakening involves that world, which reflects some of the deception characteristic of her family and none of its efficiency.

She finds the business world, the world of her husband and his colleagues, wasteful and self-aggrandizing.

> Kate kept thinking, like a housewife, of the telephone bills for all these postponings and suggestings and mind-changes; what was being spent on telephoning alone would be enough to feed thousands for weeks: but she was not being paid to think like a housewife, something less was being asked of her. (32)

The economy and efficiency and care she maintained in the family world are nowhere represented in this business world. Yet into this kingdom, her children must find their way; here "her Michael" finds a center and an identity their home does not provide.   Unable to find sustaining personal value in her job, Kate Brown scrutinizes anew her life in the family, in conventional language and society.

Of course, Kate Brown's family and the established orders

---

* This resembles the United Nations and allows Lessing, a former Marxist, to review "this new class, the international servants" who enjoy an unsettlingly lavish life while discussing world starvation.

encourage her to let sleeping dragons lie. Self-deception seems, in fact, not merely tolerated but promoted by convention. Kate Brown recognizes how she has, herself, inculcated a modicum of convention and deception in her children:

> Their behavior had been, in fact, the equivalent of the old phrases, a convention which people did not know how to lose in favour of the truth—whatever that was. (12)

Life within the conventional castle, with conventional children and husband, seems to the exiled Kate Brown both her true sphere and an isolating, exhausting place. Freed unwillingly from its hold, she faces her diametrically opposed memories about the family.

She feels nostalgia and longing for "the picture or image of herself as the warm centre of the family" (52) but admits that the recall is both romanticized and dated. Remembering the children's calling themselves "the monsters" allows her admission of having felt, at times, "like an animal teased by cruel children" (98). Her metaphors of family life astound her with their force and implied violence:

> During those years when she felt as if she were locked forever in a large box with four perpetually exploding egos, she had consoled herself with: But nothing's being hidden, everything's being said. (88)

But, in facing her memories squarely, she admits that this sustaining hope for "nothing's being hidden" has been quite disappointed. Quite like social language and public histories, the family has constructed rigid patterns of deception, of official memory. That record seems objective and reliable while hers seems subjective and suspect. She specifically recalls one shattering dinner in May during which her youngest child, Tim, accused her of smothering him. She remembers the family's falsifying that event, she, too, had longed to forget, to restructure "the incident so it could take its place among her official memories" (90). Based on fear of how devastating this remark is, they all created "a family folie," a grand "form of self-deception" (87) based upon unwillingness to examine true feeling and fear of disturbing the status quo.

Kate Brown connects this collective lie not only with

false memory but, in turn, with the markedly different experience of aging between females and males. The family, to be precise, has blamed Kate's emotional withdrawal after the May episode on her menopause: a convenient lie. The incident is dismissed as *her* problem, a problem attached to her aging and her gender rather than to any problem of the nuclear unit's use of her:

> She had not started the menopause, but it would have been no use saying so: it had been useful, apparently, for the family's mythology, to have a mother in the menopause. (98)

Thus, they officially obliterate her experience as easily as preserve it. The family falsifies its public records, its history. Kate Brown's once approved devotion to this unit seems, in time, to inspire only ridicule or rebellion. The fairytale images of motherhood little prepare Kate for such denigration, for such hostility.

But Lessing's novels most assuredly are not fairytales, even though her characters often ground their identities in such traditions. Her scrutiny of the conventional family constitutes nothing less than a meticulous expose of the family fable. She depicts actual violence and waste within the "nuclear unit" quite as carefully as do recent sociological studies. Lessing's characters become aware of their increasing stultification within the family; thus to Martha Quest, for example, the conventional family seems such "a dreadful tyranny" that she leaves her own daughter, hoping to spare them both the family's evils. A. B. Markow's fine, disturbing study of feminine pathology in Lessing's works summarizes this focus:[6]

> The family, regarded by the uninitiated as a bulwark against isolation, is shown by Lessing to be inimical to parents and children alike.

Given this focus, Lessing is sometimes compared with Virginia Woolf; both writers perceive "the horrors of the public world reflected in the private world of marriage."* While both writers

---

* B. H. Rigney's *Madness and Sexual Politics in the Feminist Novel* explores the works of Woolf, of Bronte, of Plath; Rigney's thesis is defended disturbingly well.

examine husbands and wives and families, however, Lessing's focus seems strategically determined by her Marxist orientation as Woolf's is not.

To be precise, Lessing examines the economic basis of the family to indicate its evils; this unit is designed to maintain a rigid social order. According to Lessing, well schooled in Marx and Engels's theories of the *pater-familias* as a proletariat unit, the economic supremacy of the male prevents social change; the family perpetuates this social order. As Kate Millet quite summarily states the problem:

> Engels's arguement that one cannot be a dependent and
> still an equal is very compelling.[7]

This fiscal dependence of women couples with the romantic programming of women and produces, according to Lessing's novels, a world bifurcated along strictly sexual lines. The woman who opts for this relative distance from earning her way and dealing in the world stays in illusion, is basically irresponsible. For example, in *Memoirs of a Survivor,* the young woman's desire for economic dependence and romantic love vitiates her ability to directly influence the world: she loses "the initiative she would need to be a leader of a commune. She wanted no more than to be the leader of the commune's woman. His only woman, of course" (108). The longing for male authority couples with a longing for fiscal security. This performs, in Lessing's works, a kind of emotional lobotomy on female and male alike. In turn, they perpetuate the proletariat family unit and the social status quo.

Nor are Lessing's conventional females innocent of the world's greed, stasis, wars, and corruptions. They perpetuate economic dependence and the romantic ideal to protect themselves against creating a new order. Thus Maureen, the double for Kate's daughter Eileen in *The Summer Before the Dark,* cannily reviews her suitors on two fronts: their world views and their economic potential. She can select the male whose view seems the most authoritative and whose skills seem the most marketable; she finds identity through him:

> What was becoming stronger every minute, his need that
> Maureen should stand by him and give him her support,
> could be felt encompassing her. (214)

The female abrogates any responsibility to deal directly with the world, influencing the world indirectly through the male and her children (usually her male children). In Lessing's novels, this romantic illusion that the protecting male will arrive to order the female's existence has reduced the world's ability to change by half. In this attitude, she is less an ardent feminist than an avid Marxist, although the two theories need not be diametrically opposed, of course.

The family in *The Summer Before the Dark* enforces the status quo; Kate Brown's offspring maintain appearances quite as diligently as their parents. The family has distorted certain events the better to preserve this old order. Thus both family and language mitigate against Kate's coming into knowledge. With each approach to such candid recollection, she distrusts herself. With each recall, she admits having effaced certain incidents; what she could not efface she has, as the family has, distorted. The official memories collide with her personal memories. So ingrained are these socialized, approved patterns that Kate Brown finds her faculty quite muddled; she must deliberate whether the family's falsity is more true than her personal recollection:

> Was there something wrong with her memory perhaps?
> It was seeming more and more as if she had several sets of
> memory, each contradicting the others. (52)

Like the protagonist in Margaret Atwood's *Surfacing*, however, Kate Brown pursues true memory and admits responsibility for her life, even for its delusions. Because memory is identity, to distort one is to distort the other; Kate Brown, dressed in no more protective a garment than a dress "off a rail marked Jolie Madame," assails the dragon of memory despite injunctions against this act. In this necessary confrontation, Kate Brown finds kinship with other Lessing protagonists.

Memory seems, in fact, a salient technique for characterization in these novels. For the Kate Browns and the Martha Quests, re-examining memory constitutes what Martha calls "a salvage operation" essential to reclaiming the self. Through memory, for example, Martha integrates her childhood knowledge of the social deceptions of adults with her adult embrace of these deceptions. She remembers her childhood self calling:

". . . remember, remember, remember, but she had been sucked in, she had become a coward and liar like the rest" (494). Society exerts real pressure in the distortion of personal memory, yet memory remains a faculty of personality. Because memory involves volition and selection, in fact, Lessing considers it a revelatory faculty.   Nor is she, obviously, alone in this supposition; writers from Proust (*Swann's Way*) to Hellman (*Pentimento*) would heartily agree with Lessing's declaration that "a personality is very much what is remembered."[8]   To alter or salvage memory, then, is to do the same for identity.

Kate Brown's memory undergoes an intense examination as she reviews her official identity for the past twenty years. "A woman" is in transition because she faces a mid-life crisis that is *not* the menopause. She is in transition because her child-bearing and child-rearing years are behind her and the future seems not so very promising. In transition, too, are the traditional female identities and the modern female redefinition of same. This is a typical Lessing woman, rather neatly defined by Sydney Janet Kaplan in her provocative *Feminine Consciousness in the Modern British Novel.*[9]

> . . . her female characters are caught in the middle of an evolutionary stage where there is conflict between the old expectations for women and their dysfunction in the world they live in.

Kate Brown suspects, to amplify this idea of redefinition just a bit, that her devoted motherhood had provided few of the advantages she ideally worked toward; her dismissal from the garden indicates that her fate must follow a social program that the aging woman fade obsequiously away, rather like a good soldier. And with stiff upper lip, to be sure. More upsetting is her dawning unhappiness that her years of service have produced only four more consumers, four utterly conventional citizens determined to preserve the status quo (201). She criticizes not her maternity but the institutionalization of that function; in her discernment, Kate differs from many characters who heap abuse on the individual mother rather than on the Establishment. The old expectations and the new sense of disappointment conflate in Kate Brown; that she is a fine, dedicated, discarded mother adds veracity to her inquiry at this moment of transition.

She inspires some new considerations regarding the aging woman.

So numerous and vitriolic seem attacks upon "the Mother" that a major study might evolve simply to chart the fall of the maternal star post-Bethlehem. From Freud to Lawrence to Roth, mother serves as monster and Muse. Mary Ellmann drily summarizes this phenomenon:[10]

> We are as familiar with the accusation of consumptive attachment as with the praise of selfless care . . . women are child makers and child breakers; no idea is more commonly fixed than that of the filocidal influence of the mother.

Some attacks seem puerile enough to pique interest as to whether a character's (or an author's) inadequacies must find life-long excuse in weaning techniques. From the stepmother castigated by Bruno Bettelheim in fairyland to the ubiquitous mother-in-law ridiculed by Henny Youngman, the mother seems as inexcusable a presence after forty as are children after nine in the evening. She can be ignored or jocularly reduced but must, in either case, be considered a social and personal danger to husband and offspring.

That Lessing's Kate Brown examines her own motherhood and her treatment as an aging woman proves insightful and disturbing. That the outburst regarding her smothering her son must be glossed over by the entire family is of central significance to her analysis of her life's work. That, in fact, Kate Brown demands honesty over sentimentality in thinking about her motherhood serves notice that the angel in the house is having a devil of a time and finally naming names besides her own. Kate Brown admits that "feeling guilty seems almost a definition of motherhood in this enlightened time" (98). But why is she guilty? And of what? These questions lure her into memory, into the scrutiny of her marriage and her motherhood which indicates that the social system allows her little freedom from the castle and its insistent concerns. Through memory and dream, Kate Brown studies the institution and attitudes governing conventional female identity; she finds them wanting in respect for female accomplishments within the home.

But blaming social conventions hardly constitutes escaping

them or entering into responsibility for self-renewal. Kate Brown must confront herself in order to redefine herself; this serviceable woman is neither a forthright feminist nor an acquiescing automaton (automatron?). Exiled, nevertheless, from old identities and responsibilities, she insists on reviewing her position in the world. Language and memory, despite her fear of both, guide her into knowledge.

However, since memory plays tricks to distract her attention from such scrutiny, Kate Brown needs another ally. Since dragons guard the gates of self-knowledge, Kate enters by stealth: by dreaming. Dreams of an epic journey and of a fairytale prince provide revelations about love, self, aging. Kate Brown's sleeping consciousness informs her study of language and memory; thus, her dreaming is active rather than passive. Through dreams, she gains strength of purpose and redeeming self-knowledge.

In fusing the conscious and subconscious, Kate Brown is a bonafide Lessing protagonist. Evolving dreams in *The Four-Gated City*, too, serve "as maps or signposts for a country which lay just beyond or alongside or within the landscape they could see and touch" (373 *FGC*). In all Lessing's works, dreaming is a serious business in which her characters heavily invest. For Anna Wulf of *The Golden Notebook*, dreams transform "her knowledge of herself" (408 *TGN*). Marth Quest gains insight through the subconscious and acts religiously upon such information. Dreams do more than sharpen character in Lessing however; dreams are usually a structural device which unifies each novel.

Lessing hardly invented the dream device; it is as fixed and functional a literary tool as the journey motif which, of course, also structures *The Summer Before the Dark*. From the famous Midsummer Night's Dream to Young Goodman Brown's Allegorical Reverie, the dream is, while staple fare, profoundly effective. Twentieth-century use of this device—post Jung, post Freud—seems too extensive to review. From the prophetic dreams in D. H. Lawrence's *The Fox* to the symbolic phantasms in K. A. Porter's *Pale Horse, Pale Rider,* this device is arresting. It seems as boundless, as useful and variegated as the writers' imaginations. And among her contemporaries, Lessing receives high praise for her development of this dream device.

Margaret Drabble, a novelist of considerable reputation, cites Lessing as "a great dreamer" and "a creative dreamer."[11] She remarks Lessing's ability to develop character and to fortify themes with this tool; obvious, too, is Lessing's use of dreams to unite the timeless with the contemporary. Dream symbols bridge the individual and the collective dimensions of Kate Brown's dilemma quite as effectively as does the refrain "a woman." Lessing on the economy and range of dream in *A Small Personal Voice:* "With a few symbols, a dream can define the whole of one's life and warn . . . of the future, too."[12] That Kate Brown examines past and future through dreams seems, to the avid Lessing reader, predictable, but no less exciting for that. It is rather, one might say, an interestingly predictable puzzle, like finding Nina's name in a Hirschfeld cartoon.

Kate Brown's dreams identify her, help her recognize a self obscured by years of selflessness. Two particular dreams recur, amplifying at each appearance her self-knowledge and her responsibilities. They assume epic importance and begin, in fact, "like the start of an epic, simple and direct" (29) with her exile. One dream involves an act of survival, the other, a romance. Dreams sneak her past the dragons.

In the epic journey toward survival which Kate Brown completes at the same time she completes her actual journey, she bears a lost and perishing seal northward, back to the sustaining sea. This metaphorical journey parallels her physical one. Kate Brown, in summary, leaves home and England; she travels to Turkey as an executive with Global Food, entering that experience, that identity. Then she accompanies an erstwhile lover to Spain and witnesses his physical/spiritual breakdown.* Kate Brown recovers her own psychic health alone in a Bloomsbury hotel and finishes her epic dream in the northern, dark, "cave-like" room in Maureen's flat. Thus, both in dream and actual journeys, Kate moves north, supporting Barbara F. Lefcowitz's contention that the seal symbolizes Kate's self.[13]

But this dream movement also unites major images in *The Summer Before the Dark.* Kate Brown perceives both cold and

---

* Jeffrey's crisis mirrors Maureen's and is its male counterpart.

darkness as metaphors for aging and exile. She contrasts her
outcast state with the warm family circle. Her eviction indicates
a new phase in her life, a potentially terrifying one:

> She felt, to use a metaphor she had been using, indeed,
> for some time now—as if suddenly a cold wind had started
> to blow, straight towards her, from the future. (17)

In the seal dreams, winter landscapes and darkness enclose
her and represent her fear of aging and of being alone. Yet this
dream duty to save her seal/self seems "her business" and helps
her in "wrestling with her emotional self which seemed like a
traitor who had come to life inside her" (128). Conflicting
emotions rise and subside as true memory and the dreams unite;
her quest for self-preservation develops through this dream
"like a fable or a myth" (128). To save her life, she must move
through the dark which represents on one hand the known:
her emotional conflicts as a wife and as a mother. On the other
hand, the dark suggests her long isolation from not only herself but her husband since darkness often symbolizes, in Lessing's
novels, a communication barrier between individuals. In *The
Four-Gated City*, for example, Martha Quest recognizes modern
society as "a country where people could not communicate
across the dark that separated them" (82).

Kate Brown's snow-bound, dark dream terrain represents
the lack of true contact between "her Michael" and herself.
A desolating distance, formed by long marriage and many
children and the separations imposed by social convention, has
left Kate Brown quite lonely. He hears her as a distant, in-
distinct voice quite separate from his world; when she tries to
speak, "it's as if he listens to something such a long way off it
has nothing to do with him" (245). In their traditional spheres
of influence, inside and outside the castle, the Browns live in
separate realities. ". . . he's always listening to news from
another continent. And he's never visited it nor intends to"
(245). She suffers exile and is quite alone both in the dream
and in her marriage. While she fears to progress into knowledge
and aging, she must; she can find light only through facing self-
deception and her emotional pain:

> She knew that walking into the winter that lay in front

> of her she was carrying her life as well as the seal's—as
> if she were holding out into a cold wind her palm, on
> which lay a single dried leaf. (131)

By dream's end, the seal returns to the sea and Kate to her household; she sees "the sun in front of her" (241) and the only light that fails is "the light that is the desire to please" (243). The years of selfless service are over.

This epic journey symbolizes Kate's willingness to continue her life, to change. The sea represents her subconscious knowledge, of course. And it represents, on a simple level, the unity of life and death, the temporal and eternal. To return the seal to the water seems a resurgent symbol of her personal rebirth and unification with an ancient, archetypal One. Kate Brown's journey and return to the source of life renew her.

But only through the other major dream cycle, the romantic encounter, does Kate Brown complete her knowledge of self and love and aging. This dream cycle seems sparked by memory and language as she recalls finding her prince, Michael. She uses the language of fairytales in this reminiscence; from this forty-five year old matron in exile, the language is no longer naive; it is nostalgic: "Once upon a time, she had known. . ." (66). In retrospect, her romantic illusions about love and marriage seem cruel. She remembers her girlhood training in this fantasy expectation of the prince's kiss; she feels "tempted to cry out that it had all been a gigantic con trick, the most monstrous cynicism" (91). Kate Brown recalls Kate Ferreira, her virginal and dreamy girl-self, as "a fatted goose," prepared unwittingly for the altars of romance. Kate Brown suspects that her girlhood treatment presaged the loneliness of her present exile:

> She was sheltered and distrusted. She was precious and
> despised. She was flattered by deference to her every
> wish—but knew that she, the female thing—occupied a
> carefully defined, minor part of her grandfather's life, as
> his wife had done, and his daughters. (17)

In dreams, she must meet the prince again but with the consciousness of a forty-five year old woman. In her first encounter, therefore, she equates finding the prince with assuming certain obligations. She cannot approach sexual pleasures, for example, without accepting the responsibilities socially defined as hers. She recognizes the symbolic import of the dream immediately: ". . . the dream's flavour was still, was more and more, that of another time: myth, or an old tale" (101). It seems both personal and collective; it could be any woman's dream. Like a Gretel or a Goldilocks, Kate Brown's dreaming self happens upon a cottage in the forest; the season is autumn and the hearth embers are nearly extinguished, symbolically enough. Within, the prince awaits her on the second floor.

Before ascending to him, she must attend to rather unromantic chores. She seems more Aschenputtel than princess as, neither delighted nor complaining, she prepares food, cleans the cottage, attends to:

> . . . the people in the house who, she knew, were her family, but transformed and transfigured into myth creatures, larger than themselves, representing more than they were in ordinary life. (101)

Through accepting the maintenance of castle and children and prince, "a woman" ascends to him who remains apart, above all this.

Thus, Kate Brown begins to unravel the romantic illusion which joined her to her prince and separated them, almost simultaneously. The prince, she sees, presides over but does not engage in castle business. So, too, "her Michael" has maintained, "a degree of involvement" which affords him an enviable distance from the children now that the children are grown. The female, rather than the male, has provided "a strong fixed point" around which the children have moved, now deriding, now desiring that fixed point. The prince's detachment draws a rebuke from neither wife nor offspring; he remains somehow "not really implicated" in those family follies because "he worked so hard, had so little emotional energy left over to give to the family" (87).* Given his duties to the kingdom, this distance seems approved. His connection with the castle is

---

* She admits, with difficulty, that his adulteries deplete his energies, also.

more fiscal than emotional since the care of men and children remains, according to this conventional family's operating code, the exclusive duty of the female.

Bettelheim finds this emotional distance inculcated by fairytales; his theory of the division between females and males seems quite sound. He reviews parenting expectations as defined and advanced through fairytales. According to Bettelheim, the prince never anticipates children; the princess, conversely, requires them. Their responses to parenting, therefore, conflict. As Bettelheim notes:

> As in most fairy-tales, the little boy's ideal is just he and his princess (Mother) their needs and wishes taken care of, living by themselves and for each other forever.[14]

The prince, for all his ability to kiss the princess in an utterly transforming manner, finds the appearance of children rather unexpected. Kate recalls Michael's difficult accomodation to *her* added responsibilities: the "wrench in her habits" called child-care.

> It was true that to continue living as if there had been no changes, with the wakings in the night, and the having to get up early, and the always-being-bound to the infant time-table had been hard. (91)

The princess is suddenly caught up with other egos and other duties than his and her mutual joy.

The basic problem is an identity crisis, of sorts. The prince remains a prince; the princess turns into—not a frog of course—a queen mother. So when Kate Brown remembers their doomed, slightly comic attempts to ignore the radical changes enforced by parenting, she states flatly: "Anyone could have told them this was nonsense" (91). That no one *did* accent the social adherence both to the initial romantic illusion and its necessary dissolution. But both the prince and princess find such changes difficult:

> It was extraordinary how long this couple continued to think of all these extraneous objects, cars, house, and so on, as having nothing to do with them personally—not for their sakes at all, but only because of the children. (91)

She must tend to her "true spheres," and he must earn their needs. The bifurcation of prince from princess is assured.

While he expects, through his fairytale lessons, a life-long lover to mother to his needs, and is disappointed in this hope, the female expects the encompassing love of her prince and her offspring. She, too, must suffer disappointment. As Kate's dream indicates, she accepts responsibility for prince, castle, children; this, according to Bettelheim, reflects female conditioning projected through fairytales. The princess, according to his theory, believes that conferring fatherhood upon the prince guarantees "happiness ever after."

> The little girl knows that children are what bind the male even more strongly to the female. That is why in fairytales dealing in symbolic forms with the oedipal wishes, problems and hardships of a girl, children *are* occasionally mentioned as part of the happy ending.[15]

Oddly enough, while Bettelheim emphasizes the conflicting expectations, he examines no contrary effects on female or on male. Kate Brown does.

She must sometimes subordinate "her Michael's" needs to those of the children; she must always subordinate her needs to both. She remembers "not making love with Michael when a child was ill" much as, in the dream encounter, she cannot approach the prince until finishing her chores. Since the offspring are hers, her "true sphere," the male can feel neglected at times; the female notes these tensions and attempts to assuage everyone's tempers. In this, Bettelheim finds the female properly conditioned toward self-abnegation. This is a central tenet of identity for the conventional female: such a quality leads her to the "supreme female identity" in the shift from princess to queen mother:

> The queen . . . does not try to satisfy any of her own desires, but worries about others who depend on her. . . This shows that she has successfully made the transition from wife to mother, and thus, she is reborn to a higher plane of existence.[16]

Perhaps. But conflict must ensue since this conditioning

separates beloved from beloved, female from male.

The problems Kate Brown detects in this conventional conditioning are many; the divisions apply, of course, to the conventional marriage and—with its assignation of roles—the marriage of the Michael Browns is surely that. First, the sexes do not perceive parenting the same; their notions, in fact, conflict. Fatherhood does not transform the prince's identity but does inconvenience him. Whether children therefore bind the male more closely to the female or merely tie them both up seems debatable. Nor is fatherhood the summit of his masculinity; he must scale peaks quite outside the castle for that. Conversely, motherhood transforms the princess physically and permanently. Bearing is required for her if she wants to be an approved, certified woman.

Both the fairytale identities and the social norms gloss over the rather sinister implications of sex conditioning. Prince and offspring compete for the female's attentions; thus divided, female energies must fall. The father-child rivalry, which Kate perceives unwillingly between Tim and "her Michael," receives tacit endorsement socially. Some might expect Freud's famous observation of this tension and its deleterious effects might encourage society's removing the conditions which promote it. To find and name this problem only to endorse it seems irresponsible and another indication that social mores badly need change.* To continue affirming this jealousy as a socially justifiable and scientifically certified fact makes it seem immutable; this seems infantalizing indeed. The costs to male, female, and offspring bother Kate Brown as she inventories her marriage and her motherhood. The pressures upon her seem doubled.

But an even more subliminal change divides prince from princess through fairytale gender identities. Kate's pain on recognizing this alteration is keen; the prince, "her Michael," has an alternative to the castle: the kingdom. Given his inculcated expectation for undivided attention, the prince finds a ready solution since the kingdom abounds in princesses. Thus,

---

* The "new" nurturing male is no newer than the "new" female; both have simply kept low profiles and remain "exceptions."

Michael has explored new horizons sexually and professionally while for Kate "anything that was not a child seemed a horizon too distant ever to be reached again" (92). These two have been programmed to part; Kate Brown's fairytale language is both lamentation and accusation:

> Once upon a time she had known that her husband's life had been sustained by her, by what they found together, and the centre of that was bed. (66)

The centre, the discovery, the faithful coupling have shifted, were programmed to shift.

This dragon of infidelity so terrifies Kate that only her most courageous examination of memory, coupled with her second dream encounter with the prince, allow her to confront it. After reading letters from "her Michael" who is consulting in the United States, Kate Brown seeks sleep "to lose her miserable need for her husband" (142). She enters the forest again, finding a village dominated by "the young king; he whom she had met in the wooden house where she had laid down the seal while they made love" (143). (Note how the dreams cross!) The details of this dream are crucial to Kate's dawning awareness of self, love, aging.

The king has "grown older" since their last encounter; he kisses her and, thus "claiming her," whirls her onto his elevated platform. The prince/king is always above; they dance to the adulation of the populace and what follows, again according to Lefcowitz's study of this novel, "offers a strong evocation of the plight of the aged woman in a sexist society." The king abruptly leaves her, "taking by the hands a young girl." Kate's dreaming self departs in "a desolation of grief" only to be hounded down by the villagers and thrown into a pit. The angered king approaches her weeping, dreaming self and chastizes her publicly "For her lack of generosity, her niggling and critical spirit, her failure in communal feeling, but above all, for her lack of understanding the laws that govern life" (144). The king, he icily informs her, must dance with every princess; this is expected.

Kate begins to examine these "laws that govern life." What she examines is nothing less complex than her entire romantic education, her exile, the double standard, and the

sequential infidelities which have ironically supported what Kate
calls the "real marriage" of the Michael Browns. In Kate's
retrospection, the prince's kiss seems suddenly as much a sedative
as an aphrodisiac:

> For it was seeming more and more as if she were just
> coming round from a spell of madness that had lasted
> all the years since that point in early adolescence when
> her nature had demanded that she must get herself a
> man (she had put it more romantically then, of course)
> until recently, when the drug had begun to wear off.
> (126)

The admission that the prince/princess nexus sedates rather than
awakens the female is not a new one for Lessing's females.
    The kiss which symbolizes the sexual awakening of the
fairytale female seems a rather mixed blessing even for the most
conventional females. Thus, the old women, Mrs. Quest and
Mrs. Foster, watch the young lovers and young marrieds
thinking: "Yes, but they don't know, do they? It was like a
curse, or a spell" (266). And Anna Wulf of *The Golden Notebook* considers romantic love, in fact, "the birth of naivete"
(211). Her fictional Ella, in fact, is a Galatea designed by Paul
and lulled into a false sense of both security and identity:

> Paul gave birth to Ella the naive Ella. He destroyed in
> her the knowing, doubting, sophisticated Ella and again
> and again he put her intelligence to sleep, and with her
> willing contrivance. . . (211)

Romantic love is detrimental; it is anesthetizing ecstasy to some
Lessing females who willingly abrogate any self-definition. Lynn
Sukenick seems correct in citing that Lessing allows little pity for
the female in this situation:[17]

> It is, in fact, because her heroines like men so much,
> and because they make such good Galateas of them-
> selves, that they must be so careful. It is woman's vul-
> nerability rather than man's culpability that is stressed. . .

Caught in this round robin of shifting identities and changing partners, both females and males seem somewhat mad to the exiled Kate Brown: ". . . the whole thing, crazy, men and women, both, we're all mad, and don't know it" (127). She defines her madness as that of "a prisoner of her memories," and Michael's madness as his sexual imprisonment: his being "engaged in—not so much eating as sampling a box of chocolates, taking a bite out of one, swallowing another, discarding a third without tasting it" (127). So crazed, thus imprisoned, adulteries and betrayals seem reasonable expectations.

Kate Brown tries repeatedly to shrug off the consequences of extra-marital affairs: "Perhaps," she attempts early on, "we all make too much of this kind of thing when we are young—the little affairs, you know, they are of no importance in a real marriage" (12). But this official language or prescribed reaction does not serve; according to her renascent memories and her second dream, such transgressions have altered the relationship of the Michael Browns. Yet, as a liberal couple, they have anticipated such trespasses, have forgiven them in advance, as it were. They exchanged, she recalls, "blueprints of psychological observation, or, if you like, manifestos . . . of marriage" (20). She remembers being thus prepared for infidelities, conditioned to shrug them off or to accept them as a necessary test of a "real marriage." But her true feelings refuse standard definitions; rage and contempt surface:

> . . . here was a lie, another, False memory again. She must consider, honestly, the place infidelity had had in the successful marriage of the Michael Browns. (62)

Kate Brown ponders whether this double standard and the tacit approval of such actions might have rather far-reaching, sinister effects. Of course, such social attitudes divide women into convenient camps as wives and as mistresses. But, she fears, there is more to fear here than the division of the whole woman from the whole man. Divided, too, is the male's emotional and physical sensibility; a schizophrenia, of sorts, seems to threaten the male identity. This fear seems parallel to the Surfacer's fear

in Margaret Atwood's novel* that such facile separation may
encourage increasingly mechanical attitudes: the body may do
things for which the heart is not responsible. Atwood's character
muses that:

> If the head extended directly into the shoulders . . . they
> wouldn't be able to look down at their bodies and move
> them around as if they were robots or puppets. . .

Kate Brown senses the dangers of this dissociated sensibility
in "her Michael." Backed by social custom, Michael "had
allowed her to understand" that he was having "occasionally,
and discreetly, and with every care for her, the wife's dignity,
affairs with young women who would not be hurt by them"
(63). These small hungers differ from his banquets with her,
the chosen; this very distinction unsettles rather than soothes
Kate Brown. As he trivializes these acts and the women involved
in them, he trivializes her. Not a towering passion but a sexual
dalliance leads him from their centre and union in the romantic
ideal.

> She would have preferred him to confess—no, insist, as
> his right, on a real emotion—a real bond with some
> woman, even two or three women, which would deepen
> and last and demand loyalty—from herself as well. (64)

This potential schizophrenia for "liberated" men and
women bothers Lessing's women, even those who are—as Kate
Brown assuredly is not—worldly wise. Molly and Anna, for
example, review this division in a discussion with Richard of
The Golden Notebook. Like custom, language seems to separate
the emotional and physical sensibilities (and this tradition has
been a male rather than a female one). Richard is suffering
from sexual malfunction. Bemoaning his inability to attain
erection with his wife, Richard calls the problem "a purely
physical one" and "one problem you haven't got." Molly seems

---

* The following quote from *Surfacing* (p. 91) announces the protagonist's struggle to unify head and heart, physical and spiritual.

taken aback by his distinction. "Physical, you say? Physical? It's emotional." Richard, with a stock, biological rejoinder, dismisses her remark: "No? Easy for women."* Molly's retort focuses on the split between female and male conditioning: "No, it's not easy for women. But at least we've got more sense than to use words like physical and emotional as if they didn't connect" (*TGN* 31). Anna and Molly, while carnally knowledgeable, have insisted on emotional connection.

And physical/emotional bifurcation agitates Kate Brown more than her "free women" counterparts because she is dedicated to unselfish love, to actualizing the ideal marriage. She herself has attempted Michael's sexual freedom; she has failed. Part of the failure she attributes to her still resonant love for her husband; part of the failure she attributes to a lack of opportunity. Her only flirtation terrified her because her heart and body felt precariously aligned. Second, the January-May affair was "marvelously frustrated by circumstance. . ." (66). The female, Kate admits, lacks opportunity and time; the full pressures within the castle make a chastity belt quite unnecessary: "One has to be a married woman of thirty-five with a husband and watchful children to achieve circumstances where a kiss has to be enough" (67).

She does not consider "her Michael" a morally reprehensible fellow simply because she cannot enjoy similar sexual trespasses. She even accepts her social conditioning regarding her dis-ease with adultery attempts:

> For one thing (of course literature and all sorts of experts,
> marriage counselors and the like, could have told her)
> if a woman is attuned well and truly for one man, then a
> new one doesn't come so easily. (For which reason she
> had never been able to believe in the easy pleasure of
> wife-swapping and amiable adultery). (100)

Thus, she has accepted unquestioningly the social prescriptions for female fidelity, male sexual pleasure. She does not find this conditioning divisive until she scrutinizes memory further. Be-

---

* His remark also assumes female, sexual passivity.

cause she has considered "her Michael" a prince among men, she fights against losing respect for him. Her judging him at all upsets her; she castigates herself as does the prince in the dream, using the same terms, even. Calling herself "stupid," "un-sophisticated," and "ungenerous," she accepts that society supports Michael's actions. She finds—indeed expects—no support for her feelings of betrayal, loss, rage:

> She felt about him . . . against all reason and what her
> carefully constructed blueprints told her she could feel—as
> if he had lost his way, had lost purpose. (64)

That Kate Brown feels betrayed by the romantic illusion which binds her but not her lover pulses through this novel. Her wanting to be approved, feminine, conventional has sounded the death toll for both princess and prince. Her securing pedestal power has removed her from the lover and led to her betrayal.

In her poignance and anguish, Kate Ferriera Brown seems more an innocent betrayed, more an Elizabeth Bowen character, than one of Lessing's infamous or famous "free women." And given Kate's loss of emotional innocence occurring rather late, perhaps a quick parallel with a novel by Bowen may seem not at all facetious but may indicate, rather, that Lessing does follow an established tradition in denouncing the romantic illusion. After all, both Lessing and Bowen study the emotional ideal and the emotional real. Both use memory and metaphors of exile as their characters confront self-knowledge and the social norms. And their characters suffer politely as well as profoundly. They suffer a death of the heart which paralyses the will to love, in some, and the will to live in others. As in Lessing's novels, the betrayed sentiments and ideals alter Bowen's characters perma-nently. The change is sometimes visible, sometimes invisible.

In Bowen's masterful *The Death of the Heart* (1938), for example, social language and false memory hide emotional injuries, even though the character's left ventricle is, meta-phorically speaking, severed from the right. A parade of such walking wounded—from Anna Quayne to Major Brutt to Portia, the protagonist—advances through Bowen's novel. The emotional reality seems grotesque. Violation of one's sentiments or one's fidelities constitutes an unutterably final loss; emotional betrayal kills something central and worth protecting:

> That betrayal is the end of an inner life, without which
> the everyday becomes threatening and meaningless.[18]

The hope of realizing an emotional ideal blinds Bowen's characters, obscures the very real, social forces marshalled against realization of the ideal.

When this social force finally strikes the character, the recognition is alienating. Bowen employs a metaphor of this realization perfectly applicable to Lessing's Kate Brown because it is a metaphor of exile:

> At the back of the spirit a mysterious landscape, whose
> perspective used to be infinite, suddenly perishes; that is
> like being cut off from the country forever, not even
> meeting its breath down the city streets. (320)

Characters like Kate and Portia do not risk the heart again and anyway, the wench is dead. In this study of romantic expectations and social reality, Lessing and Bowen not only create emotionally innocent protagonists but employ similar techniques.

Like Lessing, or vice versa, Bowen weaves memory so that the past and present emotional capacities and expectations of each character have a point-counterpoint. Memory serves as both balm and bane:

> Memory is quite unbearable enough, but even so it leaves
> out quite a lot. It wouldn't let one down as gently as that
> if it weren't more than half a fake—we remember to suit
> ourselves—if one didn't swallow some few lies, I don't
> know how one would even carry the past. (226)

This sounds like Kate Brown after her awakenings; it is, rather St. Quentin from Bowen's *The Death of the Heart* lecturing the devastated Portia on emotional resignation, on the required self-deceptions. For both authors, false memory obfuscates true feeling; the betrayed heart seems a *rite d'passage,* a condition necessary to social service and maturity. The romantic ideal, in fact, seems for both writers a rather monstrous and lethal notion.

Through the use of similar metaphors and techniques,

Lessing and Bowen obviously belong to the same tradition.
While writing domestic novels, however, their foci differ in-
structively. Bowen is quite simply a consummate novelist of
manners. Her works focus on the immediacy of the drawing-
room reality rather than on the larger political and social dramas
which influence Lessing's characters. Even in *The Summer
Before the Dark,* a remarkably conventional drama for Lessing's
opus, she cannot avoid broad issues like world hunger and
economic determinism. To be precise, Bowen's plots and
personae seem less obviously determined by Marx than by
remarks at high tea.

And while Bowen's characters inure themselves against
subsequent emotional betrayal—in one ineffectual way or
another—Lessing's protagonists usually insist on facing both
the ideal and its betrayal, trying quite often to figure how
they themselves are culpable. Lessing's characters, rather than
Bowen's, insist on tracing true memory and true feeling although
they suffer for their insistence. In short, the loss of innocence
and betrayal of the romantic illusion in Bowen's world is e-
motionally fatal; absolute conformity follows. In Lessing's
world, such fearsome experiences provoke personal development.
And yet, both authors recognize, to use a Lessing phrase, that
such awesome knowledge changes the emotional life: "habit
of loving" is broken.

Both Bowen and Lessing note that admissions of emotional
loss and destroyed illusions are actively discouraged by society.
Official language mitigates against such utterance; social
deceptions refuse to acknowledge such betrayals. The romantic
illusion is protected because it promotes and preserves the
existing order. To Kate Brown, the hidden clauses in the
romantic contract seem increasingly transparent. In fairytales
and the social language and unspoken custom, the double
standard wedges the female from the male. The prince succumbs
to pressures within the castle. Sexual conditioning separates
them; they are taught different modes of conduct, different
ideas of trespass and of keeping faith. Children divide them.
Love and age, "these facts that govern life," find different and
conflicting definition for the female and the male. In her second
dream, Kate clarifies her growing perceptions about these conditions as the aging male dancer selects maiden after maiden.

While this prince has aged noticeably since their previous

encounter, he continues to select younger partners (143). He discards Kate, the dancer who has aged as he has. Custom admits for the male rather than for the female, Kate avers, that "Ripeness is all." To her has not been issued the famous Browning invitation to "come grow old with me." Michael is waging a battle against time itself; Kate may be too old to dance; "her Michael" is not, although he is, in point of fact, seven years her elder. While she colors her hair and fights to retain her figure, Michael changes his hair style and mode of dress. In this society, both sexes fight the dragon of aging, and for the prince, rather than for the princess, several reincarnations seem approved:

> —when he came back from abroad somewhere the first time, having tried to turn the clock back by at least fifteen years—she had suffered a fit of trembling anger and disgust. (64)

Like the aging monarch in her romantic dream, Michael both accuses and convinces her "that she was being envious: it was petty of her." She must accept his rejuvenations as uncritically as she does his adulteries. Time, like the children, severs male from female; their treatment by time is, to some measure, socially defined. The social myths, that is, differ radically, while the female supposedly loses her sexual identity, the male pursues his ever more fervidly with middle age.

Writers other than Lessing, of course, examine this neat social paradox. Mona Von Duyn's complicated, witty, ascerbic, accurate "The Fear of Flying"[19] analyzes this phenomenon poetically. Both Lessing and Van Duyn note that, while the female is dismissed as menopausal, the male faces no such reductive shibboleth. Van Duyn notes the male's timely reincarnations: the "four parts you play." He can play "the cool, brittle, disillusioned roue," or attempt "the whole green youth bit again, the breezy,/twittery, dancing boy-girl/approach." The aging male may also project himself as the "fatherly lover" or as "the sensualist." Van Duyn's persona, rather like Lessing's Kate Brown, laments not her lover's aging but his attitude toward it and the social attitudes which separate them. She laments his posturing, longs for his timely, recognizable presence. Witnessing his varied poses, the wife notes the cultural disparity in their experiences of time; she is one whose "one-and-only springtime/in one of yours is over."

This may sound like sour grapes; it certainly does to Michael. But it is also a damning, sadly astute observation on sex-related discrimination. And more, the whole issue of fearing age indicates to Kate Brown an awful, doomed narcissism.* She notes this natural process in our artificial preventatives; both sexes spend enormous time and money on escaping time. Kate notes her appearance early in her exile:

> A woman stood in front of large mirrors in many shops
> looking with a cool, not entirely friendly curiosity at a
> woman in her early forties. . . (34)

"A woman" reviews herself in the glass, always critically. Enormous effort has produced what Kate calls "this artifact" (35).

During her exile, Kate Brown suffers a deep spiritual crisis which directly affects her physical appearance. Confronting a mirror after her illness, she finds "a woman all bones and big elbows" whose eyes are "anxious" and whose "rough mat of brassy hair" surrounds a "white sagging face" (141). A band of grey "three fingers wide" splits her head in two. In the attempt to return to her own acquaintance, to find the natural woman within the "artifact," Kate Brown undergoes a physical change quite as dramatic as that experienced by Atwood's surfacer; the "new centerfold." Knowledge of how she honestly looks at forty-five years of age is finally hers; Kate Brown confronts that dragon: fear of aging.

Attending a performance of Turgenev's *A Month in the Country* highlights for Kate her former and present attitudes toward aging. Earlier, Natalia Petrovna's preoccupations with love and age had seemed "the mirror of every woman in the audience who has been the centre of attention and now sees her power slip away from her" (155). Natalia, like the former Kate Brown, believes that her physical appearance *is* her identity;

---

* Bettelheim scrupulously avoids discussing male narcissism although the complex is mythologically ascribed to the male.

that her beauty is her power. Bettelheim states that the fairy-tale female identity promotes this notion that a woman's appearance constitutes "her worth."[20]   This partially accounts for the female's awesome reactions to time's alterations; Kate recalls her days in the looking-glass: ". . . had she really spent so many years of her life—it would almost certainly add up to years!—in front of a looking glass? Just like all women" (161).

By facing herself in the mirror and out of the mirror, she reflects on her life anew, as it were. That narcissism prescribed by fairytales as the aging queen raves against the passing of her power, her beauty, loses its hold on Kate Brown. She need not fear the youthful, albeit fleeting loveliness of Maureen or Eileen as must an aging queen mother trapped in social identities. Kate Brown confronts the dragon of time and, in so doing, makes aging her ally. Her wide river of grey is nothing less than a streak of her new nonconformity. By refusing to preserve that assiduously dressed red hair, Kate Ferriera Brown asserts some control over her appearance. The grey may seem a little act, the changing of a hair style a rather pitiful rebellion. But considering her complete conventionality before exile, her action is daring indeed. It signals a change so clearly that even her family—gifted in delusion and avoidance—must note it.

> Her experience of the last months, her discoveries, her
> self-definition; what she hoped were not strengths, were
> concentrated here—that she would walk into her home
> with her hair undressed, with her hair tied straight back
> for utility; rough and streaky, and the widening band
> showing like a statement of intent. (244)

She rejects more than the socialized "look" for the fashionably aging woman. She rejects appearances.

To appear an efficient and eminently respectable wife and mother, Kate Brown has carefully maintained the socially con-doned appearances. "The clothes, hairstyle, manners, posture, voice of Mrs. Brown (or of Jolie Madame, as the trade put it) had been a reproduction," she admits to herself (244). And she notes her former fear of seeming different; she has adhered scrupulous-ly to this model because "the slightest deviation . . . had caused her as much discomfort as the scientist's rat feels when the appropriate levers are pushed" (244). From such conditioned definitions of the aging woman, she is free. Other conspiracies with appearance demand her acknowledgment. To preserve the appearance of a serene marriage, Kate has refused to face the impact of adulteries. To protect the children from her own, natural appearance, she "always had scaled herself down" (8).

For Kate Brown, the self-scrutiny now involves more than superficial criticism of her make-up or her hair. She understands the nexus between the desire for an approved, fairly stereotyped physical appearance and its internalized values which, according to her candid feelings, lack integrity emotionally and spiritually. These admissions cost Kate Brown some false dignity but authenticate her real, lost self to the reborn middle-aged woman she becomes by the end of her exile. She escapes fear of time and of appearances which stifle her.

She is free at last to confront the one figure throughout the novel who has refused appearances. To do so, she recalls the one other fairytale figure prominent in the awakening of Kate Brown: "The Emperor's New Clothes." This tale may seem detached both from the romantic illusion and the female identity but, according to the unconventional Mary Finchley, has everything to do with both. It well may be that Mary Finchley—rather than Michael Brown—finally destroys Kate's romantic illusions. She is Kate's alter-ego, as eccentric as Kate is conventional. While she lives across the street, enjoys the same socio-economic advantages, is a wife and mother, Mary Finchley is less a reflection of Kate Brown's life than a distorting mirror. Yet the "ghost of Mary Finchley," Kate admits, accompanies her in exile. Like the seal and the dancing prince, Mary Finchley represents something strategic. Kate Brown admits that she must try to decipher this significance, "to understand what Mary meant to her, what she was standing for" (94).

To find a character serving as alter-ego or as the double in this novel, of course, seems predictable in a Lessing work, but no less remarkable for its predictable presence. In *The Golden Notebook*, of course, Molly and Anna "seem to be interchangeable." Anna creates an alter-ego in her fictional Ella of the Yellow Notebook. By manipulating Ella's romantic dissolution, Anna analyses her own relationship with Paul and prepares herself for a descent into madness with Saul Green. In *The Four-Gated City*, of course, Lynda is both double and mentor

for Martha Quest.*   That Mary Finchley informs Kate Brown
about her own identity seems quite within the Lessing tradition.

Kate's first awakenings with social languages occur with
the irreverent Mary Finchley.   Those "cow sessions" indicate
to Kate Brown just how little Mary is controlled by social
limitation and definitions.   Mary finds social restrictions quite
as preposterous as social language.   For example, she refuses
to submit to what she calls the "tyranny" of children.   Whereas
Kate "did not allow her appearance to bloom, because she had
observed early in the children's adolescence how much they
disliked her giving rein to her own nature," Mary dresses as she
pleases (225).   And whereas Kate pines for the unadulterated
attentions of just one male, "her Michael," Mary finds little,
in fact no, enjoyment in restricting her amorous appetites to
"just one man" (226).   And whereas Kate Brown in youth
selected the comely Michael for unrealistic, romantic reasons,
Mary Finchley avers choosing Bill "because he had a better job
than the rest" (225). While Kate Brown concedes that economic
security accounts for most marriages, she is unsettled by Mary's
candor:

> . . . a lot of women may think that, but they'd say Be-
> cause I loved him the most or because I admired him or
> because he was sexy. Not Mary. (225)

"Not Mary" echoes throughout this novel; the world according
to Mary Finchley seems quite as peculiar and revelatory and
controversial as any according to Garp.

Her ready admissions of economic reliance on Bill and the
exchange of services involved deplete Kate's fervor for her
romantic illusions.   She examines her economic dependence
on the good doctor even as she laments his career commitment.
As an over-paid executive with Global Food, Kate finds little
satisfaction in her economic independence longing, instead,
for the old limitations and roles.   In this, Markow's commentary

---

* Rigney rather brilliantly parallels Bronte's Bertha with Lessing's
Lynda as the "mad" wives in her *Madness and Sexual Politics in the
Feminist Novel.*

on "The Pathology of Feminine Failure in the Fiction of Doris Lessing" seems sadly applicable:[21]

> The source of their failure is dual: they do not feel the
> need to assume responsibility for themselves, and they
> are deeply, but wrongly, committed to romantic love,
> the two being causally linked.

Kate's emotional ties prevent her free movement from former dependencies; her nostalgia for the old compact drags her backwards, even as her exile and self-knowledge pull her forwards. To Mary Finchley, romance figures less prominently in her decisions than reason: she trades her freedom from economic responsibility for Bill's freedom from child-care responsibility. Kate Brown finds the anti-romantic Mary Finchley a frightening conundrum, one which she fears to solve.

Yet the supposition that the female does not choose judiciously strikes the canny Mary as wild self-deception. Unlike Lessing's conventional, self-sacrificing women, Mary refuses the romanticization of marriage and motherhood. She does not accept that her gender leaves her "no choice but to sacrifice herself." The Mrs. Quests and Kate Browns believe in their duty to the family and to the romantic dream. They recognize their exaltation and desecration as necessary forms of their sainthood and martyrdom:

> As in a romantic novel or a fairy story, she saw her self,
> wayward beauty, flirting with this one and that one, then
> bestowing herself: I, your despised mother, gave myself
> to your father, your grandfather—your existence is the
> result of my choice. (250) *The Four-Gated City*

Such conflicting sentiments elicit in Mary Finchley only a shrug or a laugh. She cannot comprehend why the choice of a husband thereafter extinguishes the desire to choose again and again, sexually. Nor does she place herself last, behind the needs of husband and children. She cannot identify, as can Kate Brown, with a normal woman shopping for her family's needs:

> She moves away, bowed down, weighed down, a slave,

> her shoulders saying how satisfying it was to bear burdens
> for others. (175)

But Mary Finchley, unbowed and unbossed, finds this image ludicrous instead of praise-worthy.

Mary Finchley is no princess; she's not even much of a queen mother. She is most certainly not the Madonna of "not my will but Thine be done." Nor is she an Eve, expiating guilt for curiosity and disobedience through service. She is, rather, a bit of Lilith, refusing to behave, refusing to obey, insisting on her own will. Mary refuses the double standard. As a wife, for example, she refuses marital fidelity, finding it as unwholesome and inconvenient as the wandering prince does. She considers the promise of marital bliss through sexual restriction "the world well lost for lust" (36). Nor does she engage in the subterfuge and discretion which characterize Michael's affairs. She brings her lovers into her house; Bill, having divorced and remarried Mary, admits that "after Mary, he couldn't really take to a woman." While her sexual appetite bothers him, he accepts that "she's very immoral, but she's wonderful apart from that" (227). For her part, Mary Finchley finds this judging of her sexual habits much ado about nothing. Both Bill and the conventional community seem to her irrational:

> . . . they were operating from two different sets of laws.
> He had divorced his bad, vicious wife who was corrupting
> the children, but she was the victim of a crazy man.
> "Well, what's the matter with you?" she kept saying.
> "We get on all right." (227)

What society outside defines as correct or moral simply exerts no influence on Mary Finchley.

And Kate Brown's theory of the dissociated sensibility in "her Michael" needs revision in light of Mary Finchley. Unlike Kate, Michael and Mary feel no uneasiness in enjoying the bodily delights. Love matters less than sensation; fidelity matters less than fun. Mary Finchley cannot provide solace for Kate Brown's suffering because Mary thinks the idea of sexual restriction is simply ridiculous. Bill should expect no such thing from her much as Kate must, Michael informs her, expect no such thing from him. Mary enjoys what seem to be traditionally male

prerogatives in attaining her own sexual experiences and satis-
factions.

Further, she is more male than female in her attitude
toward parenting. Mary Finchley is the only woman of Kate
Brown's acquaintance who remains untamed. She has refused
the education of her peers: women. All women have "a long
education in just one thing, fussing" (93). But Mary does not
fuss; she is untrainable. And, discouragingly enough for a devoted wife and mother and fusser like Kate, neither Bill nor
the children seem the worse for Mary's nonchalance. Mary's
children, in fact, are quite like Kate's; they are infinitely more
conventional than their mother Mary. Kate says that "guilt"
is the major component of the mother; not Mary:

> She hasn't any sense of guilt—that's the point. We are all
> in invisible chains, guilt, we should do this, we mustn't
> do that, it's bad for the children, it's unfair on the hus-
> band. (225)

Mary is abnormal; the whole conditioning program set to
separate the sexes breaks down before the intrepid Mary Finchley. The double standard and the romantic illusion are quite
literally lost on her. In this distorting mirror, Kate Brown
sees her own life pursuit of appearances, of approval, of some
feminine image as perfect wife and mother as the goals of "a
raving lunatic" (229).

> An unafraid young creature had been turned, through
> the long, grinding process of always, always being at other
> people's beck and call, always having to give out attention
> to detail, minuscule wants, demands, needs, events, crises,
> into an obsessed maniac. (94)

Such maniacs are created, according to Mary Finchley, by
romantic delusion. The romantic conventions and attendant
restrictions are the living enactment of "The Emperor's New
Clothes." She considers romance a collective phantasm, designed and perpetuated by frightened women and frightened
men:

> . . . she really believes that the way everyone goes on

> about love, being in love, is some sort of conspiracy, the
> emperor has no clothes. (226)

Free of guilt, free of the will to please, free of appearances, free
of an identity based on self-abnegation, Mary Finchley imperils
the romantic illusion precisely because she suffers few ill effects
from avoiding it. She makes an equitable pact with a nice male;
she maintains her human prerogatives and refuses to dress up
her actions "emperor style" with layer upon layer of romantic
angst. No calling toward the sacred duty of women calls Mary;
men and children are included in the pact she has made. Here
neither Kate nor Maureen can find reinforcement that women
civilize the world, that altruistic women exchange sympathy
for an unromantic world. This woman defies romance and
sanctimonious interpretation of her life, a life which accepts
marriage without appearances of "happily ever after." Mary
Finchley's story helps Kate Brown shake off the tranquilizing
effects of the prince's kiss and her conformity:

> Love, and duty, and being in love, and not being in love,
> and loving, and behaving well, and you should and you
> shouldn't ask and you ought and you oughtn't. It's a
> disease. (229)

Mary Finchley, for satisfying her own needs, for mini-
malizing her parental obligations, and for refusing conventional
dress and behavior, is considered mad. For assuming that male
prerogatives are human prerogatives, she scandalizes Blackheath.
During Kate's descent into madness and memory and two dream
epics, however, Mary Finchley's eccentricity reflects a new
sanity. As so often in Lessing's works, madness is a lucid
rebellion. But the insights of the mad terrify those of us
vigorously adhering to defined orders, to socialized sanity.

So Mary Finchley's story terrifies Maureen, who faces the
decision of whether and whom to marry. Mary's story robs
the romance, loots the ideal marriage dream. Marriage is an
economic fact and Maureen will marry to escape monetary
responsibility for herself and to settle her restless pursuit of an
identity. Through marriage, she can attain identity as a wife
and, soon after, a mother; her purposelessness need not depend
on her finding a personal and possibly unconventional identity.

Maureen can have all that Kate Brown has sought: prince and children and castle.

Like Eileen, Maureen represents the daughter of the seventies who repeats her mother's life without the mother's belief system. Kate Ferriera Brown has believed in the "true sphere" notion; the women of Maureen's generation want to believe but are caught in a transitional time. Maureen's nostalgic request that Kate "tell her a story" of joy in being a wife and mother signals her partial distrust of the romantic illusion and the sexual divisions.

> The nostalgia is a concomitant of the social transition in which women are caught with their emotions lagging perceptibly behind their intellectual perceptions.[22]

Maureen refuses any self-definition beyond the old order; because she does not take her self seriously, Maureen must conform. That is, she refuses to support herself; she refuses to determine her own world view and studies, instead, which of her suitors' opinions best suits her. The two images which surround Maureen in dreams and in waking are of a caged yellow bird and a doll. By novel's end, Maureen has changed her hair, as has Kate. Maureen snips off her golden tresses and weaves a hair doll. She selects the richest of her suitors and gives herself a farewell party: "But her guests had been greeted by the hair doll, not by her." Maureen follows the conventional bridal path; Kate Brown surveys the terrain ahead of this young woman:

> One could easily imagine them together, in their large house in Wiltshire or somewhere, deep in plentiful horses, children, and dogs, everything according to pattern, including their humorous comments on it. (247)

Kate Brown, unlike Maureen, summons the will to change and to admit the lessons of her experience. Her exile seems a fortunate fall into knowledge: memory and dream help her to pursue and find her self. Exile opens regions beyond the home and homeland and prescribed identities for Kate Brown. The journey into knowledge is neither pleasant nor easy; it is beset by monstrous admissions and fearsome dragons. But, like her

nineteenth-century counterpart, Edna Pontellier, Kate chooses personal truth and personal awakening:

> The years that are gone seem like dreams—if one might go on sleeping and dreaming—but to wake up and find— oh! well! perhaps it is better to wake up after all, even to suffer, rather than to remain a dupe to illusions all one's life.[23]

Without the sedating romantic illusion, Kate Brown faces the actual sacrifices and joys and humiliations involved in her womanhood and motherhood and marriage. Her collusions with society seem, from the perspective of Kate's exile, the machinations of a madwoman in a mad world. That "Love is a woman's whole existence" and the "youth is the best time of one's life" assume, for the awakened Kate Brown, monolithic proportions as she sees the waste of human potential. Without individual change, her daughter and sons must undergo the same severe recognitions which—in time—alter Kate's attitudes toward convention.

Her descent into knowledge deepens Kate's understanding of self, love, and aging. The hero confronts her social and personal fears; she slays the dragons. Lessing's protagonists re-activate the will, a human function almost completely stifled by sexual conditioning. Lessing asserts in her introduction to *The Golden Notebook* that "A woman's way of looking at life has the same validity as the filter which is a man's way." The quest for knowledge is a human one and the courage to confront self-delusion a human quality. Lessing notes, in her introduction to *The Golden Notebook* that her transcriptions of "what many women were thinking, feeling, experiencing came as a great surprise" and such novels as *The Golden Notebook* were greeted as the compositions of an "unfeminine," "Man-hating" woman. To fear such phrases is cowardice; to apply such phrases is ignorance. Lessing's females question rigid social patterns; they do so from a spirit of responsibility for the world.

Reviewing Lessing's continuing scrutiny of how language and social custom impose out-moded identities on the sexes, Kaplan aptly summarizes this gender issue in Lessing: "what is defined as 'feminine'," her books contest, is considered irrelevant to "the survival of the race."[24] This is not to say that Lessing

discounts the *value* of those aspects socially defined as
"feminine." Intuition and love and aestheticism and pacifism
remain necessary qualities in life; rather, Lessing refuses the
separation of such aspects into gender-related camps. Logic
and intuition are only through social conditioning applicable
to one sex or the other. To realize how misconstrued are concepts like aging and loving and gender leaves Lessing's protagonists, quite like the author herself, doubtless, profoundly
saddened and disturbed. That petty fears and confinements
diminish the human experience causes anguish in Lessing's
heroes from Charles Watkins to Kate Brown.

Their encounter with knowledge is never comforting; it
is often alienating. But it is the individual's duty to seek self-
knowledge and from that vantage to understand the wider
world. Martha Quest's metaphor for such enlightenment employs an image at once homely and eternal, if I recall my
Egyptian mythology correctly:

> There had been no ecstasy, only a difficult knowledge.
> It was as if a beetle had sung. There should be a new
> word for illumination. (*MQ* 53)

There should indeed. But in Lessing's canon, a proper scrutiny
of old words can also provide insight and illumination.

According to Lessing's protagonists, the human race focuses
only myopically on individual potential for being and for defining reality. Nevertheless, an adamant hope remains that the
small, insistent questions which nag at the back of her characters' minds suggest a plethora of possible answers. Certainly
exile seems a form of self-discovery; dreaming and waking
cognitions find unity. An unutterable question, a single Word:
these have fascinated writers as means of presenting awesome
and alluring possibilities for human renewal. That Prufrock
can barely insinuate his "overwhelming question" and must
torment himself with a non-conformity consisting of whether
or not to eat a peach or roll his trousers bespeaks, nonetheless,
a world of potential actions.

Possibly, a woman's questions may differ from a man's
while our conditioning remains so disparate; both genders must,
according to Lessing, move into an imaginable universe considerably more diverse than our present, dulling reality. All

Lessing's female protagonists must answer a question which is the moral equivalent of Prufrock's. Since Martha Quest seems the penultimate Lessing hero, to date, I shall quote her postulation of that question: "Mother, must I go on dancing?" Lessing piques interest as to whether answers might not prove as diverse and graceful as the motions.

Notes

[1] Doris Lessing, *The Four-Gated City* (New York: Bantam, 1969), p. 516.

[2] Doris Lessing, *The Summer Before the Dark* (New York: Bantam, 1973), p. 7. All citations taken from this text.

[3] Lessing, *The Golden Notebook*, p. 252.

[4] Lessing, *The Four-Gated City*, p. 23.

[5] Adrienne Rich, *Of Woman Born* (New York: Bantam Books, 1976), p. 32.

[6] A. B. Markow, "The Pathology of Feminine Failure in the Fiction of Doris Lessing," *Critique*, 16 (1974), p. 93.

[7] Kate Millett, *Sexual Politics* (New York: Avon Books, 1970), pp. 167-175.

[8] Paul Schlueter, *The Novels of Doris Lessing* (Carbondale: University of Illinois Press, 1969), p. 82.

[9] S. J. Kaplan, *Feminine Consciousness in the Modern British Novel* (Urbana: University of Illinois Press, 1975), p. 140.

[10] Mary Ellmann, *Thinking About Woman* (New York: Harcourt, 1968), p. 135.

[11] Margaret Drabble, "Doris Lessing: Cassandrea in a World Under Seige," *Ramparts*, 10 February, 1972, p. 50. Drabble notes that Martha Quest is a mother lode for psychological critics.

[12] Doris Lessing, *A Small Personal Voice* (New York: Knopf), p. 62.

[13] B. F. Lefcowitz, "Dream and Action in Lessing's *The Summer Before the Dark*," *Critique*, 17 (1975), p. 111.

[14] Bruno Bettelheim, *The Uses of Enchantment: The Meaning and Importance of Fairy Tales* (New York: Vintage Books, 1977), p. 112.

[15] Bettelheim, *The Uses of Enchantment*, p. 113.

[16] Bettelheim, *The Uses of Enchantment,* p. 83.

[17] Lynn Sukenick, "Feeling and Reason in Doris Lessing's Fiction," *Contemporary Literature*, 14, No. 4 (1973), p. 523.

[18] Elizabeth Bowen, *A Death of the Heart* (New York: Random House Books, 1955), p. 320.

[19] Mona Van Duyn, "The Fear of Flying," in *No More Masks*, ed. Ellen and Barbera Bass (New York: Anchor Press, 1973), p. 133.

[20] Bettelheim, *The Uses of Enchantment*, p. 202.

[21] Alice Bradley Markow, "The Pathology of Feminine Failure in the Fiction of Doris Lessing," *Critique*, 16 (1974), p. 88.

[22] Kaplan, *Feminine Consciousness,* p. 140.

[23] Kate Chopin, *The Awakening* (New York: Putnam's, 1964), p. 292.

[24] Kaplan, *Feminine Consciousness*, p. 139.

The Female Experience as Exile

Any work purporting to probe the female experience with the "forbidden fruit" must, in courtesy if not in conscience, assess the consequences of that desire. Certainly both religious and social stories, as they are usually interpreted, teach the female correct modes of behavior. Many tales, such as "The Sleeping Beauty" and "Cinderella" convince the female that the prince's kiss dispels the curse of her own curiosity. She "awakens" to prescribed dreams of fulfillment, living in his castle, on his money, under his possibly benevolent rule, praising his adventures.

If, perchance, a female fancies her ability to transform a frog into a prince, she learns early on that, in any case, he is already royalty. Woody Allen, with or without Diane Keaton, reigns as clown prince. Such fairy tale and mythic programs for the sexes convey to the male a belief in his dominion over the female and to the female a distrust of her own judgment. She fears ethical self-rule. But literature, by both sexes, examines the individual in ethical conflict and, through "ironic modification," praises the assumption of individual, ethical responsibility.

In each novel examined, previous self-concepts and expectation collide with "forbidden fruit:" knowledge of good and evil. The protagonist receives or seeks out understanding for which she must, however reluctantly, become responsible. To do so, she must violate her former training as a selfless, will-less, obedient female. Each protagonist becomes aware of culpability in perpetuating her own "freedom from" self-governance. She faces her acceptance of the possibly restrictive roles as servant of God through service to man. As princess, too, the female is removed from actual encounters with the world beyond the castle.

This moment of "non serviam" is a crucial one because in thus refusing to obey assigned roles, the female enters dangerous, undefined territory. In resisting social and religious identities, the female must create her own. That is, such a female rejects the standard Biblical and fairytale definition of the "feminine temperament, status and role," as Kate Millett notes:

> . . . femininity is her fate as 'anatomy is her destiny.'
> In so evading the only destiny nature has granted her,
> she courts nothingness.[1]

But despite the dangers of nihilism, each protagonist seeks ethical self-rule: the forbidden fruit. Elsalill confronts her hopes, hopes defined by the romantic illusion. Elsalill must violate her destiny of love and service to the prince; she must respond to a more correct destiny and responsibility than marriage. The prince, embodied by Sir Archie, holds a worldly code; he is not a benevolent prince, however, but a rapacious and amoral Soldier of Fortune. Yet, he is not the sole representative of evil; Elsalill recognizes within herself an evil: the desire to avoid responsibility for knowledge. She wishes to embrace the romantic illusion rather than to create a just social reality. Assuming the burdens of ethical judgment, however, Elsalill chooses wisely, despite the enormous personal sacrifice of love, of life. This female, gaining knowledge of good and evil, chooses good.

In Kate Chopin's *The Awakening*, Edna Pontellier obtains transforming knowledge for which she, too, must become responsible. Through contemplation of her own nature, an act directly forbidden by church fathers from Paul to John Paul II, Edna re-defines her responsibilities. Her individual freedom and self-dominion threaten to bring calumny upon her children; yet, she finds the social restrictions against her assuming responsibility for her own changes unjust.

> By all the codes which I am acquainted with, I am a
> devilishly wicked specimen of the sex. But some way
> I can't convince myself that I am. (216)

While Edna refuses to believe herself an evil woman, she recognizes her violation of social restrictions. Only to spare her children, however, does she attempt the impossible and heroic: to swim the Gulf. She refuses to abdicate self-knowledge and self-rule, preferring to face death rather than to return docilely to what she terms "the world of illusion." That is, Edna Pontellier refuses the restrictions placed against the female as wife and as mother, casting off the detritus of the romantic illusion.

Nor are ethical responsibilities less complex in Atwood's *Surfacing*. The protagonist must discriminate true from false memory, true ethical responsibility from passive reaction to her life deeds. She must recognize that her parents have taught her to prefer life and that, in rejecting them and in rejecting her unborn child, she has aligned herself with those, like David and Anna, who prefer death. That is, the abortion, for which she has blamed her adulterous lover, is her own responsibility. Against the evil of her time which romanticizes the dichotomy between the head and heart, the thought and the act, the male and female responsibility of self-governance, she must seek unity. In her "refusal to be a victim" and a princess waiting for others to defend honor and good, the Surfacer creates knowledge of good and evil, actively.

Kate Brown of Doris Lessing's *The Summer Before the Dark* attains knowledge of good and evil in the world and in herself. She searches sullenly through the emotional debris of a twenty-five year marriage to reassess who she is and what she has accomplished for herself and the world's knowledge of good and evil. She confronts the knowledge gained from her experiences within and without the castle. To serve the family is not an unmitigated good; to refuse service is not an unmitigated evil. Nothing in her romantic upbringing has prepared her for such knowledge, however. The world outside the castle, Kate discovers, promotes few of the virtues extolled within the castle: temperance, honesty, service, order. The world of convention and of business and of social diction seems false, wasteful, meritricious. Kate Brown admits her own passive complicity with this order and resolves to refine her own ethical judgments and self-definitions.

Using structural devices which seem similar (the island settings, the fairytale parallels, the "ironic modifications," and the journey), each novel examines the female under ethical duress; that is, the images of women offered by the story of Eve or Pandora or Psyche, by fairytales of a Sleeping Beauty, a Rapunzel, a Cinderella hardly project that a woman confidently define herself, seek knowledge of good and evil, and violate extant restrictions. Obedience is required of the female, not

self-governance; nevertheless, this literature celebrates the protagonist's ability to discern ethical responsibility, even if she
must sacrifice former identities, expectations, and roles. The
female becomes, in each case, responsible for good and evil.

Each of these characters meets her social opposite within
herself: Queen meets beggar and Eve meets Lilith; Magdalen
meets Mary and the Witch invites the Angel in. What knowledge of good and evil occurs, finding definition in these novels,
makes these tales of "curious" women worthwhile reading.
The first consequence of knowledge is that the seeker experiences new ethical burdens; the second consequence is that she
experiences exile.

Exile is a person; exile is a place; it provides the central
metaphor for the human experience. And exile, like knowledge
of good and evil, is sometimes sought out by the exile him or
herself. Literature is replete with their stories. Verses from
the *Divine Comedy* stamp the very Florentine structures from
which Dante was rather unceremoniously declared *persona non
grata*. This indicates that the exile sometimes laughs last. Surely
this is the case in James Joyce's scathing indictment and moving
portrait of a city and its people: *Dubliners*. To find exile celebrated seems as common in literature as to find Eve's sinful
plucking of that "forbidden fruit" celebrated.

The state of exile contains within it, possibly, the possibility
of transcendence. This seems implied in a classic of modern
theater, *A Doll's House* by Henrik Ibsen. The play is also a
model example of Welty's concept of "ironic modification."
Nora's self-imposed, utterly necessary exile from her home and
family and former identity offers her time and space for successful creation of a mature, ethical self or for failure. The outrage,
even horror, which greeted the play signals the dread uncertainty
which attends men and women regarding female self-creation.

Nora's closing of that downstairs door is the moral equivalent of Eve's moving beyond the gates of Eden. The female's
desire to transcend limitations (defined paths to salvation) seems
irrefutable. This means changes for the Torvalds, of course, who
must review their own ethical behavior. Torvald's sovereignity,
like Adam's, seems to promote an ethical indolence.

> To have a whole human creature consecrated to his
> direct service, to pleasing and satisfying him in every

way possible—this has kept the man selfish beyond the
degree incidental to our stage of social growth.[2]

Popular interpretations of exile as punitive and of Eve's
desire for knowledge of good and evil as *only* evil keep the
human race in a state of spiritual remission, at best. This, in
turn, maintains a long-perceived paradox that the daughters of
Eve are also the angels in the house. This paradox—and what it
means in terms of the female's access to knowledge—hardly
eludes Lagerlöf or Chopin or Lessing or Atwood. Their protagonists, therefore, move from these confines at great personal
risk and seek ethical knowledge.

That women might feel a sense of exile different from men's
needs some consideration. When a male is exiled from Eden,
where he has putatively enjoyed dominion, he enters another
realm in which he is still dominant. The seeking female has
suffered not only exile but calumny; thus the male may yet
exercise a punitive dominance over her. The daughters of Eve
suffer a two-fold sense of exile eloquently expressed by Virginia
Woolf in her remarkable *Three Guineas:*

> Our country . . . throughout the greater part of its history
> has treated me as a slave; it has denied me education or
> any share of its possessions. . . . For, in fact, as a woman,
> I have no country. As a woman I want no country. As
> a woman my country is the whole world.[3]

This is the garden of woman's exile, and each of the novels
examined employs metaphors of exile.

These protagonists enter exile as a metaphysical state from
which they review civilization. In each case, the judgments made
by these newly awakened Eves is ethical. Each inquires, as did
Selma Lagerlöf in a famous address regarding suffrage and equal
rights:

> Have we done nothing which entitles us to equal rights
> with man? Our time here has been long—as long as his.[4]

But protagonists realize that the answer to this question still
seems caught in the prohibitions established in Genesis and the
fairytales. Nevertheless, these protagonists accept knowledge of

good and evil; they redefine themselves. They move into exile, leaving behind the Judeo-Christian and the fairytale imperatives against female self-rule. Eve's daughters, apparently, remain willing to pay the consequences for the "forbidden fruit."

And so this presentation comes full circle, back to Eden and archetypes, to Eve and princesses, back to the issue of knowledge of good and evil. Women, according to these novels, confront knowledge and behave courageously. In the human deliberations regarding this first act and its ethical implications rests, even now, the issue of transcendence.

To awake from dreams of punitive exile, of dangerously "curious" women, of romantic illusions restricting male and female identity may demand more courage than humans possess. Given the examples offered in these works by Chopin, Lagerlöf, Atwood, and Lessing, great change accompanies the will to knowledge. The protagonists must renounce old dreams, old forms of identity, old curses and promises.

What follows such transforming knowledge? Perhaps the best summary of what awaits is that presented by Nobel poet, Nelly (Leonie) Sachs.[5] Her persona flees from the known, having gained the perilous promise of knowledge of good and evil:

> I hold instead of a homeland
> the metamorphosis of the world

Notes

[1] Kate Millett, *Sexual Politics* (New York: Avon Books, 1969), p. 177.

[2] Charlotte Perkins Gilman, "Women and Economics," in *The Roots of American Feminist Thought,* ed. Miriam Schneir (New York: Vintage Books, 1972), pp. 230-246.

[3] Virginia Woolf, *Three Guineas* (New York: Harcourt Brace Jovanovich, 1938), p. 108-109.

[4] H. A. Larsen, "Four Scandanavian Feminists," *Yale Review,* Vol. V.,

(New Haven: Yale Publications, 1916), p. 354.

[5]Nelly Sachs, "Flight and Metamorphoses," in *O! The Chimneys,*
trans. Hamburger, Holme, Mead, Roloff, Mead (New York: Farrar, Straus
and Giroux, 1967), p. 145. To free Nelly Sachs from a Nazi extermination
camp, Selma Lagerlöf enlisted the aid of the Swedish royal family. Sachs
arrived in Sweden and lived to create her Nobel-winning poems.

Appendix A

Dictionary of the Bible, ed. Joseph Hastings (New York: Charles
Scribner's & Son's 1927).

Adam: . . . man is sharply marked off as a created being from
God the Creator; and is not connected with Him
by a chain of interior gods . . . man has a certain community of nature with God; he is made in his image(P),
and receives his life from the breath of Jehovah(J). He
is lord of all things animate and inanimate, the crown
of creation(P) Woman is also secondary and subordinate to man, and the cause of his ruin, but of
identical nature. The formation of single woman for
the man implies monogamy. (36)

Eve: The New Testament teaches that Adam's being formed
first justifies that 'women must live in quiet subordination to their husbands' and that Adam was not
deceived as Eve was. (247)

Appendix B

Selma Lagerlöf: 1851-1940
Born: Marbacka, Varmland, Sweden.

1882-85	Teacher's College
1885-95	Taught school
1891:	*Gosta Berling Saga*
1894:	*Invisible Links*
1897:	*The Miracles of Antichrist*
	The Queens of Kungshalla & Other Sketches
1901-02:	*Jerusalem* (2 volumes)
1904:	*The Treasure*
	Christ Legends
1906-07:	*The Wonderful Adventures of Nils*
1909:	NOBEL PRIZE for LITERATURE
1911:	*Lilicrona's Home*
1912:	*Thy Soul Shall Bear Witness*
1914:	Membership in SWEDISH ACADEMY
1916:	*Trolls and Men* (misc.: tales, addresses essays)
1918:	*The Outcast*
1919:	*Trolls and Men* (vol. 2)
1925-28:	*Ring of the Lowenskolds* (a Trilogy)
1934:	*Marbacka*
	Memories of My Childhood (autobiographical)
	The Diary of Selma Lagerlöf

While this listing is neither annotated nor complete, it may afford insight regarding Lagerlöf's reign and productivity, range and longevity.

Appendix C:

Historical Place as Historical Value

Seneca Falls, cradle of the American Feminist Movement, has been the subject of several studies by educators, demographers, and historians all seeking to explain why this central New York community birthed so enormous a movement.

Among these studies is a work by a life-long resident of Seneca Falls, who provides an insightful detail which seems to many feminists a monumental, symbolic irony:

> As a child, I can remember twirling around the historical marker that indicated the place where the first Women's Rights Convention was held. The Wesleyan Chapel is now a laundromat with only three of the original brick walls standing.[1]

A laundromat: this is the moral equivalent of "reincarnating" Philadelphia's Independence Hall as a garage. Yet the detail seems oddly fitting, one-hundred and fifty years since the composing of the "Declaration of Sentiments." In the 1980's the letters ERA have come to mean: 1) a baseball statistic 2) the Equal Rights Amendment; 3) a detergent which can revolutionize.

Notes

[1] Carol E. Simson, "Seneca Falls: The Village and Its Women," (Syracuse University, unpublished manuscript, 1976), p. 1.

Bibliography

CHAPTER I

American Literature, ed. Walter Sutton and Harrison T. Meserole and Brom Weber. Lexington D. C. Heath, 1969.

Atwood, Margaret, *Surfacing.* New York: Popular Library, 1976.

Baudelaire, *The Flowers of Evil and All Other Authenticated Poems*, ed. P. J. W. Higson and Elliot R. Ashe. Chester: Cestrian Press, 1975.

Bettelheim, Bruno, *The Uses of Enchantment.* New York: Vintage Books, 1977.

Broumas, Olga, *Beginning with O.* Yale Series of Younger Poets, 72. New Haven: Yale University Press, 1977.

Bruns, J. Edgar, *God As Woman, Woman As God.* New York: Paulist Press, 1971.

Campbell, Joseph, *The Flight of the Wild Gander: Explorations in the Mythological Dimension.* Chicago: Regnery Company, 1972.

—. "Folkloristic Commentary." *The Complete Grimm's Fairy Tales.* New York: Pantheon Books, 949, vii-xiii.

Cheever, John, *The Stories of John Cheever.* New York: Knopf Publishing Company, 1978.

Chopin, Kate, *The Awakening*, (1899), reprinted. New York: Capricorn Books, 1964.

Daly, Mary, *Beyond God the Father: Toward a Philosophy of Women's Liberation*. Boston: Beacon Press, 1973.

deBeauvoir, Simone, *The Second Sex,* trans. H. M. Parshley. New York: Bantam Books, 1953.

Dictionary of the Bible. ed. Joseph Hastings. New York: Charles Scribners' Sons, 1927.

Eliade, Mircea, *Myth and Reality*. New York: Harper & Row Publishers, 1963.

Engels, Frederich, "The Origin of the Family, Private Property, and the State (1866)." *Feminism: The Essential Writings,* ed. Miriam Schneir. New York: Vintage Books, 1972, 189-204.

Fitzgerald, F. Scott, *The Great Gatsby.* New York: Charles Scribners' Sons, 1925.

Frye, Northrop, *Return of Eden.* Toronto: University of Toronto Press, 1965.

Fuller, Margaret, *"Woman in the Nineteenth Century."* *The Roots of American Feminist Thought*, ed. James L. Cooper and Sheila McIssac Cooper. Boston: Allyn & Bacon, Inc., 1973, 107-113.

Gilman, Charlotte Perkins, "Woman and Economics." in *Feminism: The Essential Historical Writings,* ed. Miriam Schneir. New York: Vintage Books, 1972, pp. 230-246.

Greeley, Fr. Andrew, "Pope Remains Complex Figure." *North Country Catholic,* 9 January 80, 6-7.

Haupt, C. L. "On *Transformations."* *Anne Sexton: The Artist and Her Critics*, ed. J. D. McClatchy. Bloomington: Indiana University Press, 1978.

Hays, H. R., *The Dangerous Sex: The Myth of Feminine Evil.* New York: G. P. Putnam's Sons, 1964.

Hesse, Hermann, *Demian,* trans. M. Roloff and M. Lebeck. New York: Bantam Books Inc., 1968.

Hurston, Zora Neale, *Jonah's Gourd Vine.*   Philadelphia: J. B. Zippincott Co., 1934.

Ibsen, Henrik, *A Doll's House,* trans. R. Farquhavson Sharp and Eleanor Marx-Aveling. New York: Dutton Publishing Co., 1954.

Joyce, James, *A Portrait of the Artist as a Young Man.* New York: Viking Press, 1959.

Kierkegaard, Soren, "The Fear of Dread," trans. Walter Lawrie. Princeton: Princeton University Press, 1946.

Langer, Suzanne, *Philosophy in a New Key.* New York: New American Library, 1951.

Larsen, H. A., "Four Scandanavian Feminists." *Yale Review* V (1916), 350-354.

Lessing, Doris, *The Summer Before the Dark.*   New York: Bantam Books, 1973.

Mailer, Norman, *An American Dream.* New York: Dial Press, 1965.

Millett, Kate, *Sexual Politics.* New York: Avon Books, 1970.

Milton, *Complete Poems and Major Prose,* ed. Merritt Y. Hughes. New York: Odyssey Press, 1957.

Pomeroy, Sarah, *Goddesses, Whores, Wives, Slaves: Women in Classical Antiquity.* New York: Schocken, 1976.

Rich, Adrienne, "When We Dead Awaken" *On Lies, Secrets, and Silences.* New York: W. W. Norton, 1979.

—. "The Phenomenology of Anger." *Selected Poems.* New York: W. W. Norton, 1978.

Sachs, Nelly, *O! The Chimneys,* trans. Hamburger, Holme, Mead, Roloff, Mead. New York: Farrar, Straus, Giroux, 1967.

Sagan, Carl, *The Dragons of Eden.* New York: Ballantine Books, 1979.

Sexton, Anne, *Transformations.* Boston: Houghton Mifflin, 1971.

Simson, Carol E., "Seneca Falls: The Village and Its Women." Thesis. Syracuse University, 1976.

Sochen, June, *Herstory.* New York: Alfred Publishing Co., Inc., 1974.

Stanton, Elizabeth Cady, *The Woman's Bible* (1895-98). New York: Arno Spring Publications, 1972.

Stone, Kay, "Things Walt Disney Never Told Us," *Women and Folklore,* ed. Claire R. Farrer. Austin: University of Texas Press, 1975.

Stone, Merlin, *When God Was A Woman.* New York: Dial Press, 1976.

Tillich, Paul, *The Courage To Be.* New Haven: Yale University Press, 1952.

Von Franz, Mary-Louise, *Problems of the Feminine in Fairytales.* New York: Spring Publications, 1972.

Welter, Barbara, "Something Remains to Dare: Introduction to *The Woman's Bible*, by Elizabeth Cady Stanton. New York: Arno Press, 1974, v-xlii.

Welty, Eudora, *The Eye of the Story.* New York: Random House, 1970.

Woolf, Virginia, *Three Guineas.* New York: Harcourt Brace Jovanovich, 1938.

Young, Vernon, *"Transformations,"* in *Anne Sexton: The Artist and Her Critics,* ed. J. D. McClatchy. Bloomington: Indiana University Press, 1978.

CHAPTER II

Bettelheim, Bruno, *The Uses of Enchantment.* New York: Vintage Books, 1977.

Berthoff, Warner, *The Ferment of Realism.* New York: The Free Press, 1965.

"Books of the Week." *Providence Sunday Journal.* 4 June 1899, 15.

Chopin, Kate O'Flaherty, *The Awakening* 1899; rpt. New York: Capricorn Books, 1964.

—. *The Awakening and Other Stories,* ed. Barbara H. Solomon. New York: New American Library, 1976.

Dondore, D. A., "Kate Chopin," *Dictionary of American Biography.* 1930, IV, 90-91.

Ebel, Kenneth, Introduction to *The Awakening* by Kate Chopin. New York: Capricorn Books, v-xiv.

Kolodny, Annette, "Some Notes on Defining a 'Feminist Critic.:'" *Critical Inquiry,* 2 (1975), pp. 75-92.

Millett, Kate, *Sexual Politics.* New York: Avon Books, 1970.

Pattee, F. L., *The Development of the American Short Story.* New York: Harper & Brothers, Publishers, 1923.

—. *A History of American Literature Since 1870.* New York: The Century Company, 1917.

Payne, Wm. Morton, "Recent Fiction." *Dial,* 27, No. 75, (1899), 75.

"Recent Novels," Review of *The Awakening, Nation,* LXIX, (1899), 96.

Review of *The Awakening. Nation* LXIX (1899), 96.

Rich, Adrienne, *Of Woman Born: Motherhood as Experience and Institution.* New York: Bantam Books, 1976.

Seyersted, Per, *Kate Chopin: A Critical Biography.* Baton Rouge: Louisiana State University, 1969.

Wolff, Cynthia Griffin, "Thanatos and Eros: Kate Chopin's *The Awakening." American Quarterly,* 25 (1973), 449-471.

Wheeler, Otis B, "The Five Awakenings of Edna Pontellier," *The Southern Review,* 11 (1975), 118-128.

Ziff, Lanzer, *The American 1890's: Life and Times of a Lost Generation.* New York: The Viking Press, 1966.

CHAPTER III

Arnold, June, "Introduction to the Novel." *The Treasure,* by Selma Lagerlof. Plainfield: Daughters, Inc., 1973.

Berendsohn, Walter A., *Selma Lagerlöf: Her Life and Work.* trans. George F. Timpson. Port Washington: Kennikat Press, Inc., 1931.

Bettelheim, Bruno, *The Uses of Enchantment.* New York: Vintage Books, 1977.

Brooks, Van Wyck, *The Flowering of New England: 1815-1865.* New York: E. P. Dutton and Co., Inc., 1940.

Davis, Charles E., "Eudora Welty's *The Robber Bridegroom* and Old Southwest Humor," *A Still Moment: Essays on the Art of Eudora Welty,* ed. John F. Desmond. Metuchen: The Scarecrow Press, Inc., 1978, 71-81.

Finch, Olga, "Selma Lagerlof," *Outlook*, LXX (1902), 977-980.

Gustafson, Alrik, *Six Scandanavian Novelists*. Princeton: Princeton University Press, 1940.

—. *A History of Swedish Literature*. Minneapolis: University of Minnesota Press, 1961.

Hoare, Dorothy M., *The Works of Morris and Yeats in Relation to Early Saga Literature*. Cambridge: University Press, 1937.

Howard, Velma Swanston, "Selma Lagerlof: The First Woman to Win the Nobel Prize for Literature," *Putnam's Magazine*, VII (1909-1910), 708-713.

Lagerlof, Selma, "How I Turned Scribbler," *Living Age*, 327 (1925), 322-329.

—. *The Treasure*, trans. Velma Swanston Howard. Plainfield: Daughters, Inc., 1973.

Leach, H. G., "Miss Lagerlof's Popularity," *The American-Scandanavian Review* v (1917), 113.

Martin, Terence, *Nathaniel Hawthorne*. New York: Twayne Publishers, Inc., 1965.

Melville, Herman, "Hawthorne and His Mosses," *in The Shock of Recognition*, Edmund Wilson. New York: Farrar, Straus and Company, 1943, 187-204.

"Nathaniel Hawthorne," *Cyclopedia of World Authors*, ed. Frank N. Magill. New York: Harper & Bros., 1958, 489.

Porter, Katherine Anne, *Introduction to A Curtain of Green and Other Stories*, by Eudora Welty. New York: Harcourt, Brace, and Co., 1936, iv-xvi.

Ridge, Lola, Review of *The Holy City*, by Selma Lagerlof. *American-Scandanavian Review*, VI (1918), 222.

Sackville-West, Vita, "Preface" to *Selma Lagerlof: Her Life and Work* by Walter Berendsohn. Port Washington: Kennikat Press, Inc., 1931, v-x.

Tillyard, E. M. W., *The English Epic and Its Background*. New York: Oxford University Press, 1954.

—. *The English Epic Tradition*, The British Academy's Wharton Lectures on English Poetry, XXII. London: Humphrey Mildord Amen House, E. C., 1936.

Welty, Eudora, *The Eye of the Story*. New York: Random House, 1970.

Whalen, Edward J., "The Nobel Prize-Winner," *Current Literature* 48 (1910), 218-219.

Wheeler, Edward J., "Sweden's Greatest Woman Poet," *Current Literature* XLVI (1909), 288-289.

CHAPTER IV

Atwood, Margaret, *Surfacing*. New York: Popular Library, 1976.

—. *Survival: A Thematic Guide to Canadian Literature*. Toronto: House of Anansi Press, 1972.

Bettelheim, Bruno, *The Uses of Enchantment*. New York: Vintage Books, 1977.

Bissell, Claude, "Politics and Literature in the 1960's" *Literary History of Canada: Literature Written in English*, III, ed. Carl F. Klinck. Toronto: University of Toronto Press, 1976, 3-15.

Brown, Rosellen, "Review: *Circle Game.*" *Nation* 212 (1971), 824-826.

Campbell, Joseph, *The Hero With a Thousand Faces*. The Bollingen Series, XVII. New York: Pantheon Books, 1949.

Campbell, Josie P., "The Woman as Hero in Margaret Atwood's *Surfacing,*" *Mosaic* XI (1978), 7-28.

Christ, Carol P., "Margaret Atwood: The Surfacing of Woman's Spiritual Quest and Vision," *Signs* 2 (1976).

Coughlin, Ellen, "Margaret Atwood" *Books and Arts,* 7 March 80, 5-6.

Dickey, James, *Deliverance.* New York: Dell Publishing Co., 1971.

Frye, Northrop, *Anatomy of Criticism: Four Essays.* Princeton: Princeton University Press, 1971.

—. *The Bushe Garden.* Toronto: House of Anansi Press, 1971.

—. "Conclusion," *Literary History of Canada: Canadian Literature in English,* III, ed. Carl F. Klinck. Toronto: University of Toronto Press, 1976, 318-332.

—. "Haunted by Lack of Ghosts," *The Canadian Imagination,* ed. David Staines. Cambridge: Harvard University Press, 1977.

Gibson, Mary Ellis, "A Conversation with Margaret Atwood," *Chicago Review* 27 (1974), 105-113.

Guerard, Albert J., "The Journey Within," *Modern British Fiction,* ed. Mark Shorer. New York: Oxford University Press, 1961, 110-117.

Hammond, Karla, "An Interview with Margaret Atwood," *The American Poetry Review* 8 (1979), 27-29.

Marshall, Tom., "Atwood Under and Above Water," *The Malahat Review* 41 (1977), 89-94.

Millett, Kate, *Sexual Politics.* New York: Avon Books, 1970.

Northey, Margot, *The Haunted Wilderness: The Gothic And*

Grotesque in Canadian Fiction. Toronto: University of Toronto Press, 1978.

Onley, Gloria, "Power Politics in Bluebeard's Castle," *Canadian Literature* 60 (1974), 26-42.

Pacey, Desmond, "The Course of Canadian Criticism," *History of Canada: Literature Written in English*, III, ed. Carl F. Klinck. Toronto: University of Toronto Press, 1976, 16-31.

Sandler, Linda, "Interview with Margaret Atwood," *The Malahat Review* 41 (1977), 7-27.

Sontag, Susan, *On Photography.* New York: Farrar, Straus and Giroux, 1977.

Sullivan, Rosemary, *"Surfacing* and *Deliverance."* *Canadian Literature* 67 (1976), 6-20.

Woodcock, George, "Margaret Atwood as Novelist," *The Canadian Novel in the Twentieth Century,* ed. George Woodcock. Toronto: McClelland & Steward Ltd., 1975, 312-326.

CHAPTER V

Atwood, Margaret, *Surfacing.* New York: Popular Library, 1976.

Bettelheim, Bruno, *The Uses of Enchantment.* New York: Random House, 1955.

Bowen, Elizabeth, *The Death of the Heart.* New York: Random House, 1955.

Brewster, Dorothy, *Doris Lessing.* New York: Twayne Publishers, Inc., 1965.

Brooks, Ellen W., "The Image of Woman in Doris Lessing's *The Golden Notebook, Critique* 15 (1973-74), 101-109.

Chopin, Kate, *The Awakening.* New York: G. P. Putnam's Sons, 1964.

Drabble, Margaret, "Doris Lessing: Cassandra in a World Under Seige," *Ramparts* 10 (1972), 50-54.

Elmann, Mary, *Thinking About Woman.* New York: Harcourt, Brace, Jovanovich, Inc., 1968.

Howe, Irving, *Celebrations and Attacks.* New York: Horizon Press, 1979.

Kaplan, Sydney Janet, *Feminine Consciousness in the Modern British Novel.* Chicago: University of Illinois Press, 1975.

Lefcowitz, Barbara F., "Dream and Action in Lessing's *The Summer Before the Dark,"* *Critique* 17 (1975), 110-115.

Lessing, Doris, *A Small Personal Voice,* ed. with introduction by Paul Schlueter. New York: Alfred A. Knopf, 1974.

—. *The Four-Gated City.* New York: Bantam Books, 1969.

—. *The Golden Notebook.* New York: Bantam Books, 1962.

—. *Memoirs of a Survivor.* New York: Borzoi Book, 1974.

—. *The Summer Before the Dark.* New York: Bantam Books, 1973.

Lyndon, Susan, Review of *The Four-Gated City* by Doris Lessing, *Ramparts* 8 (1970), 48-52.

Markow, Alice Bradley, "The Pathology of Feminine Failure in the Fiction of Doris Lessing," *Critique* 16 (1974), 88-100.

Millett, Kate, *Sexual Politics.* New York: Avon Books, 1969.

Rich, Adrienne, *Of Woman Born.* New York: Bantam Books, 1976.

Rigney, Barbara Hill, *Madness and Sexual Politics in the Feminist Novel.* Madison: University of Wisconsin Press, 1978.

Ryf, Robert S., "Beyond Ideology: Doris Lessing's Mature Vision," *Modern Fiction Studies* 21 (1974), 193-201.

Schlueter, Paul, *The Novels of Doris Lessing.* Carbondale: South Illinois University Press, 1969.

Sukenick, Lynn, "Feeling and Reason in Doris Lessing's Fiction." *Contemporary Literature* 14 (1973), 515-535.

CHAPTER VI

Gilman, Charlotte Perkins, "Woman and Economics," in *Feminism: the Essential Historical Writings,* ed. Miriam Schneir. New York: Vintage Books, 1972, pp. 230-246.

Larsen, H. A., "Four Scandanavian Feminists," *Yale Review* V (1916), pp. 350-354.

Millett, Kate, *Sexual Politics.* New York: Bantam Books, 1973.

Sachs, Nelly, *O! The Chimneys,* trans. Hamburger, Holme, Mead, Roloff, Mead. New York: Farrar, Straus, Giroux, 1967.

Woolf, Virginia, *Three Guineas.* New York: Harcourt Brace Jovanovich, 1938.